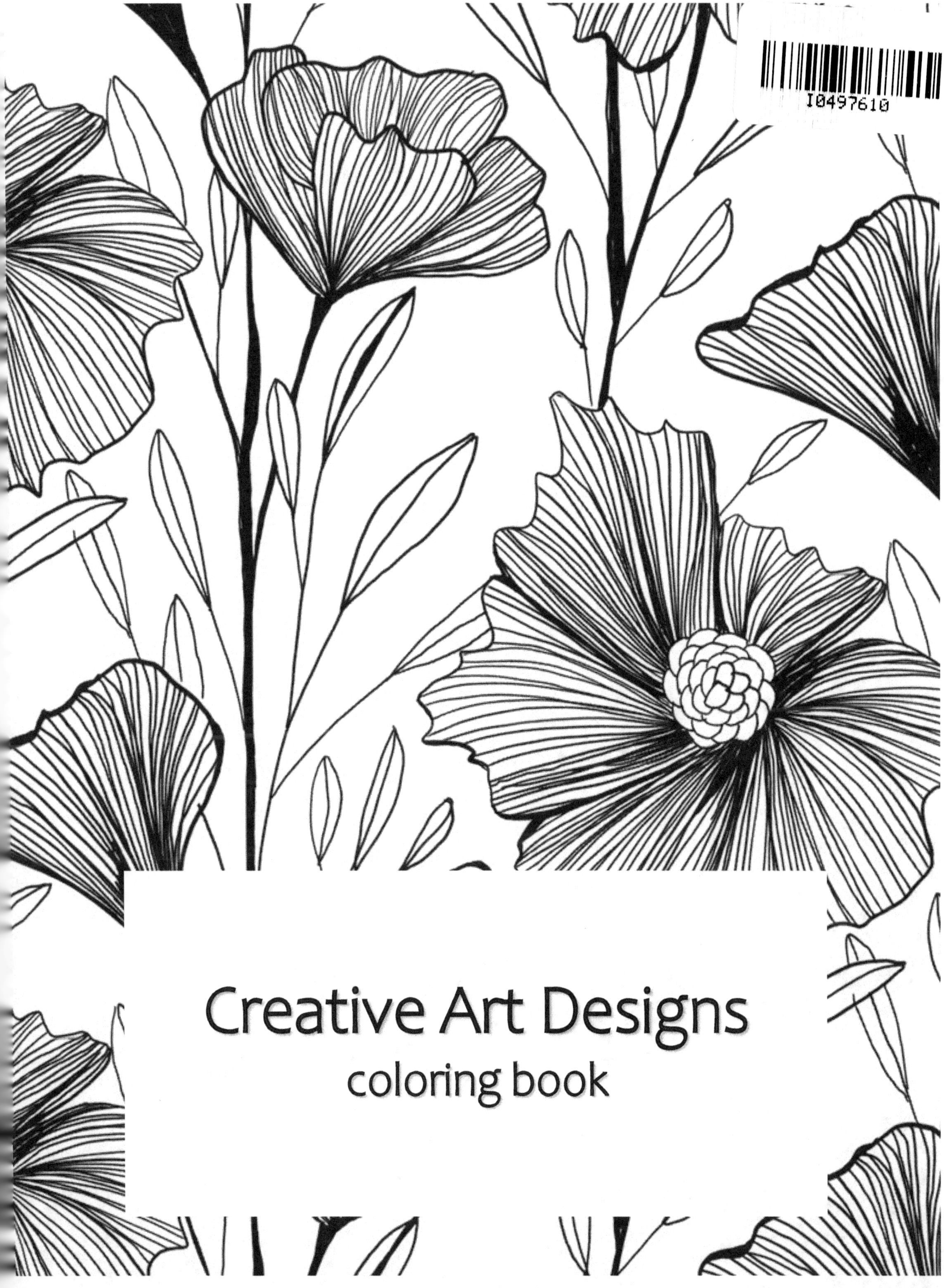

Creative Art Designs

coloring book

This book belongs to

____

____

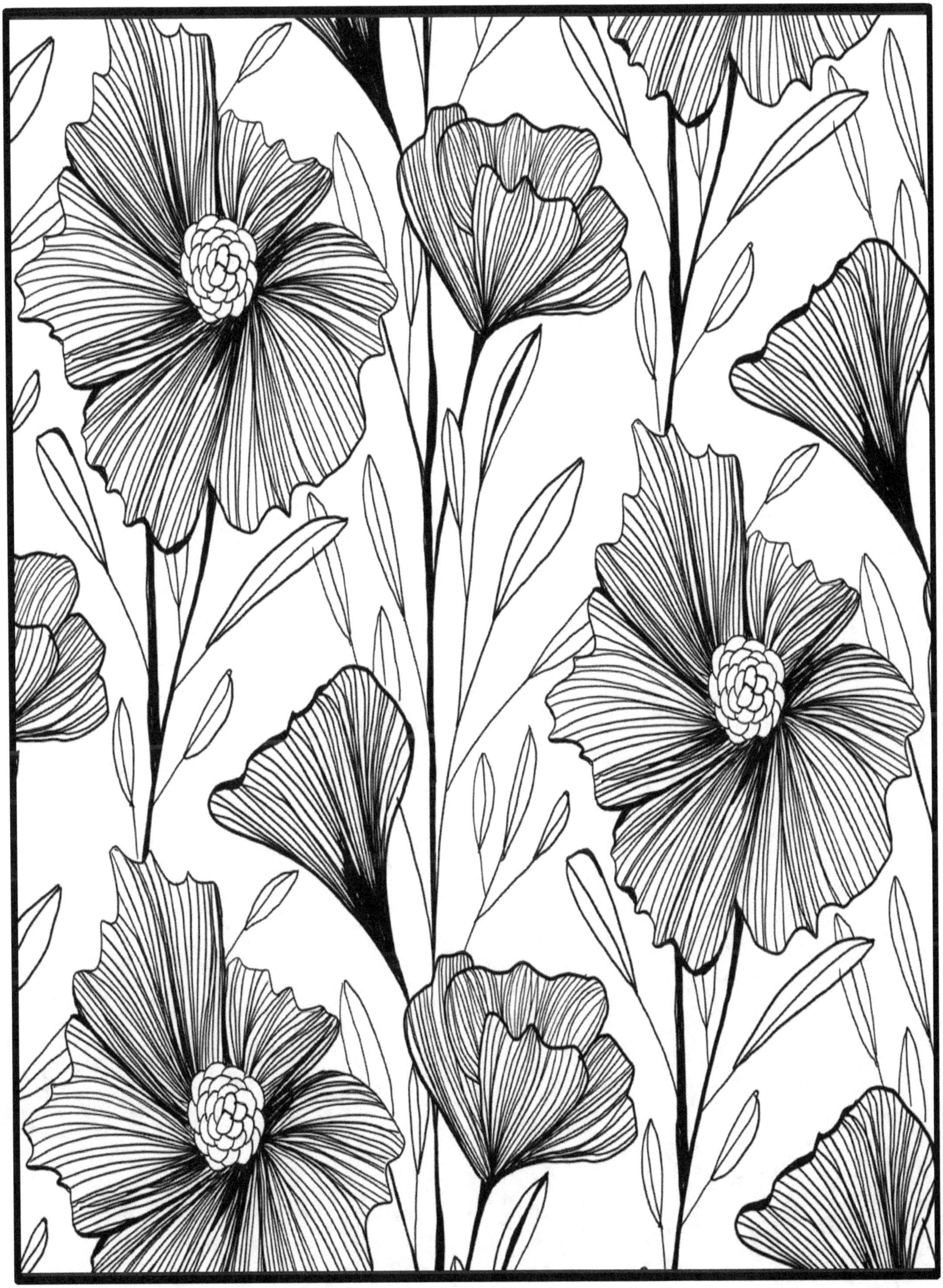

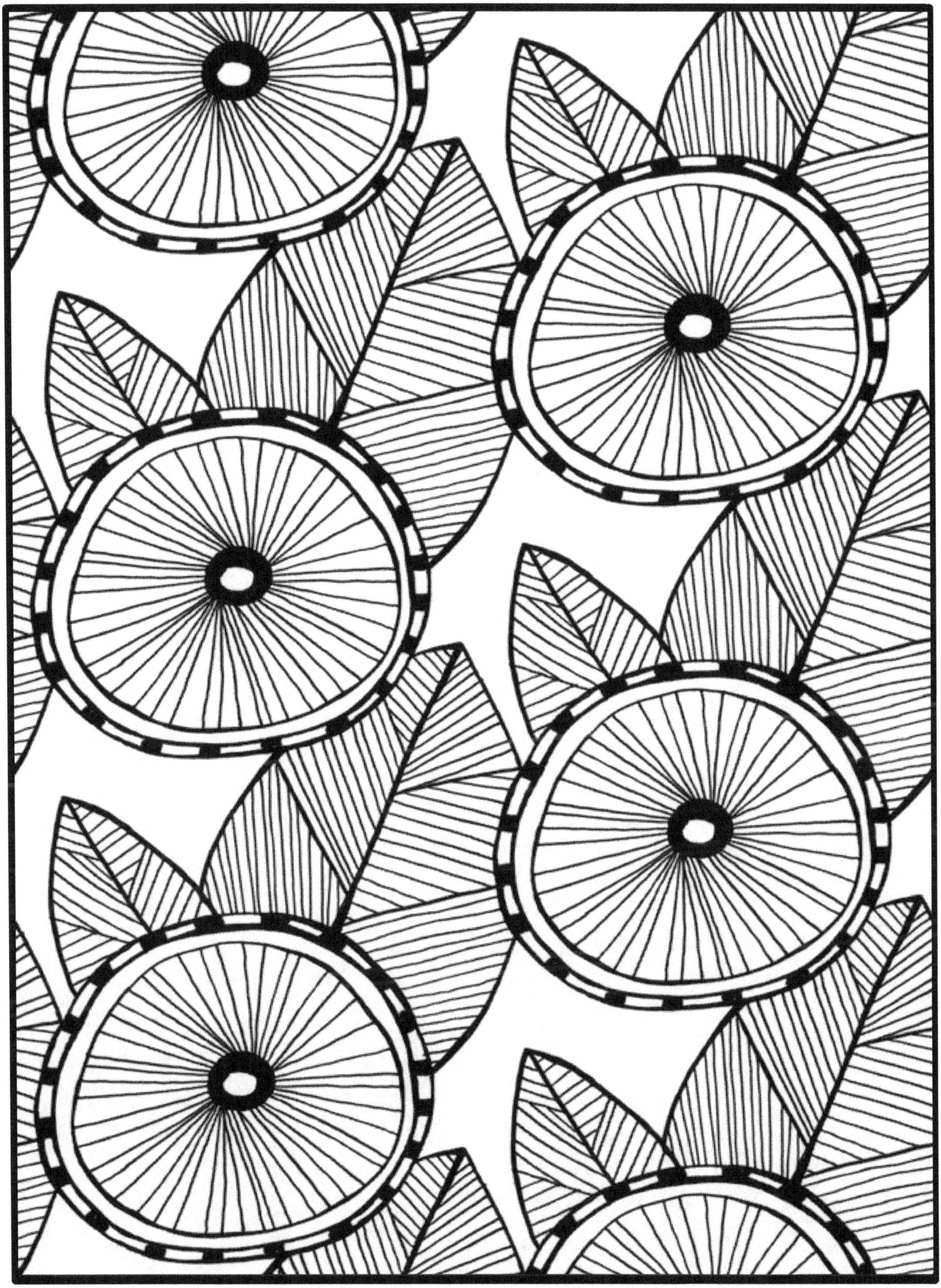

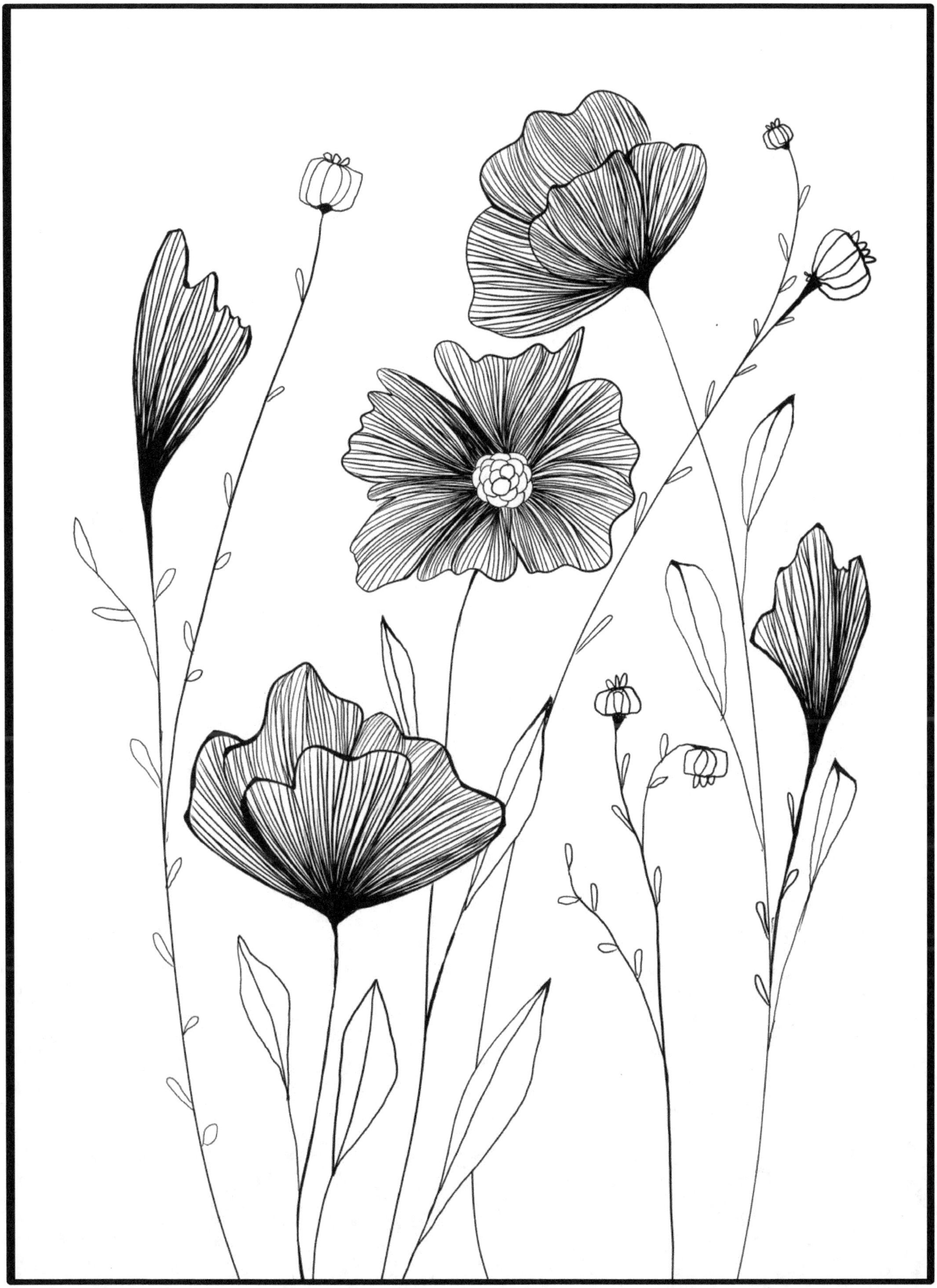

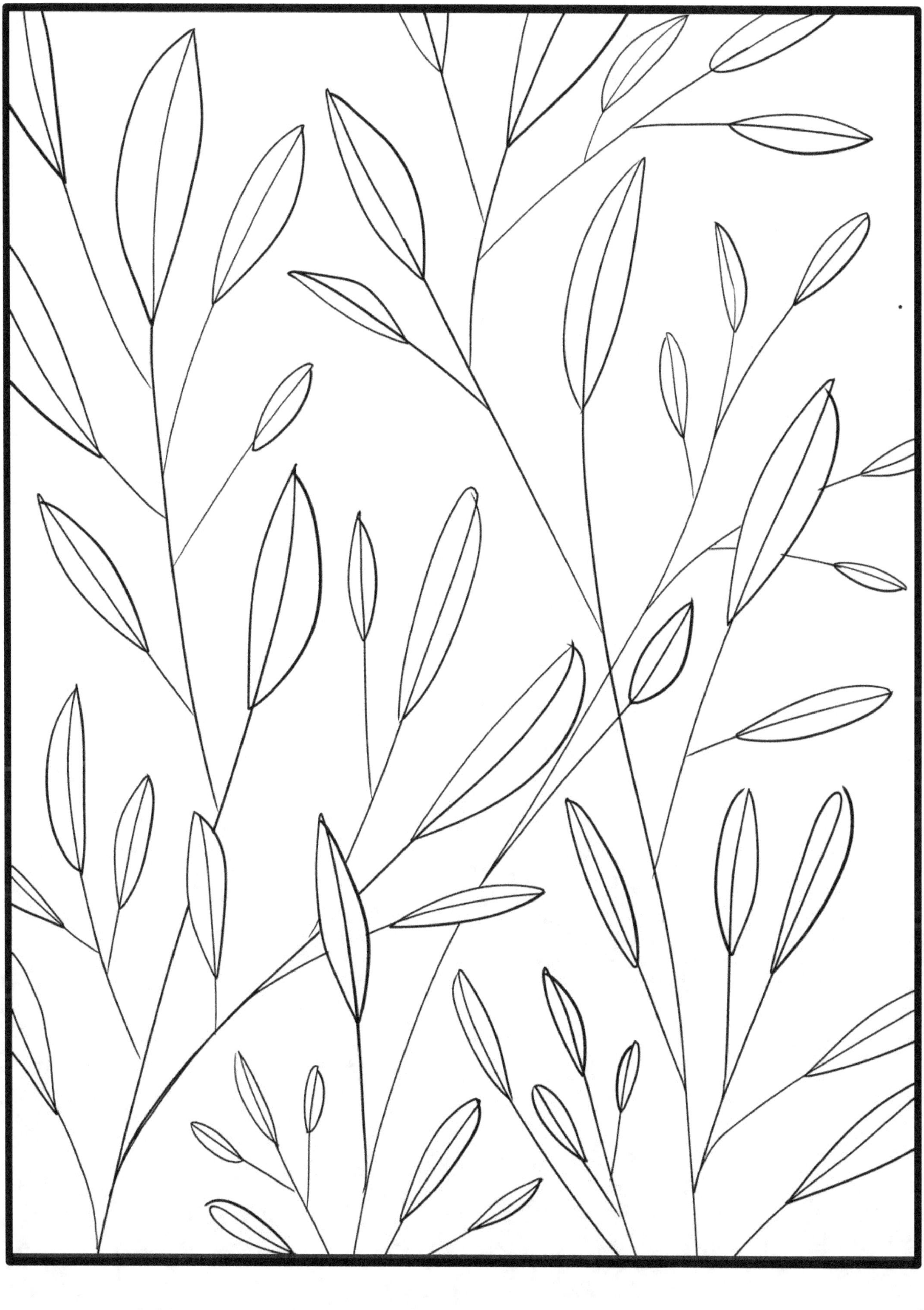

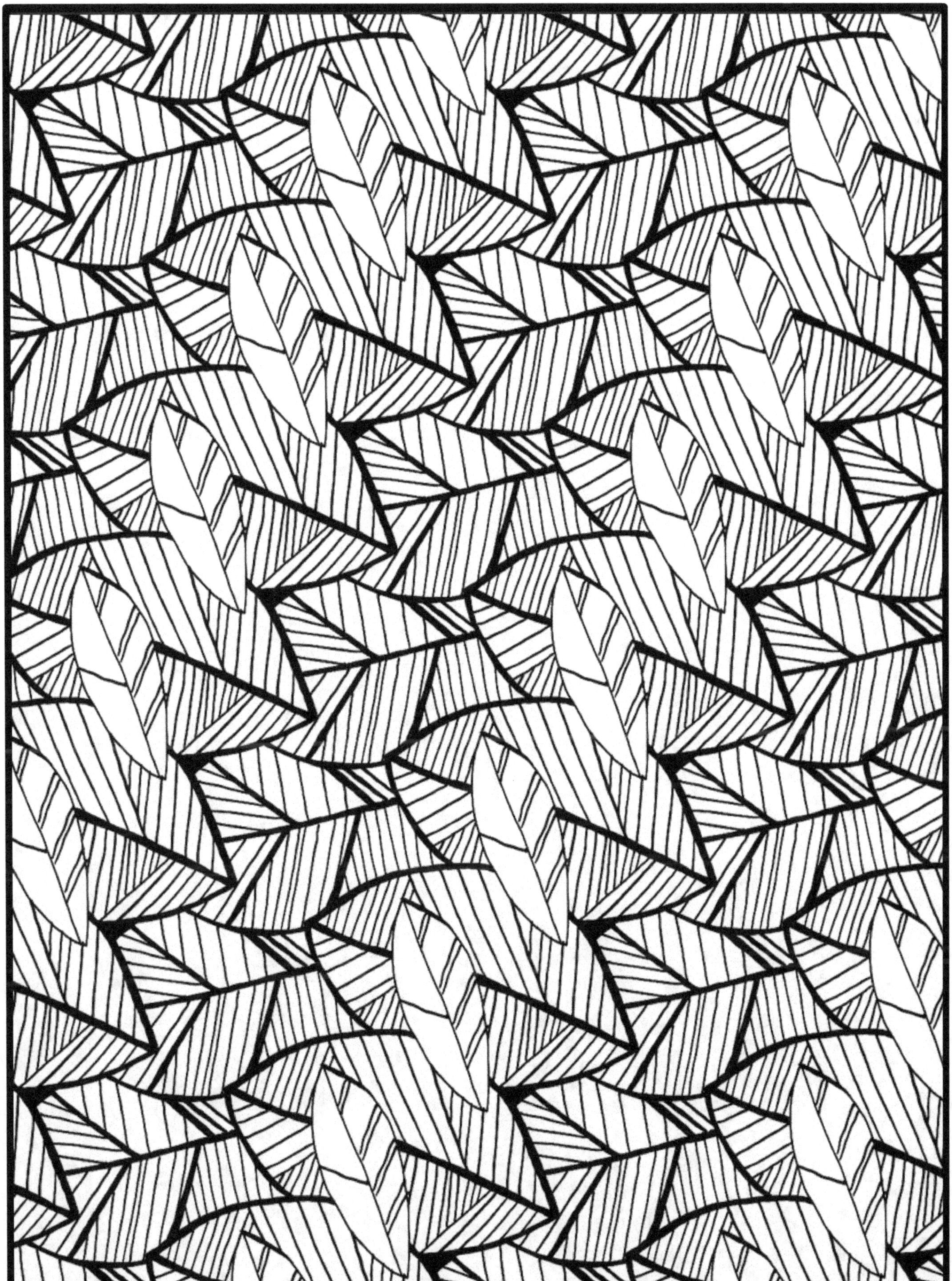

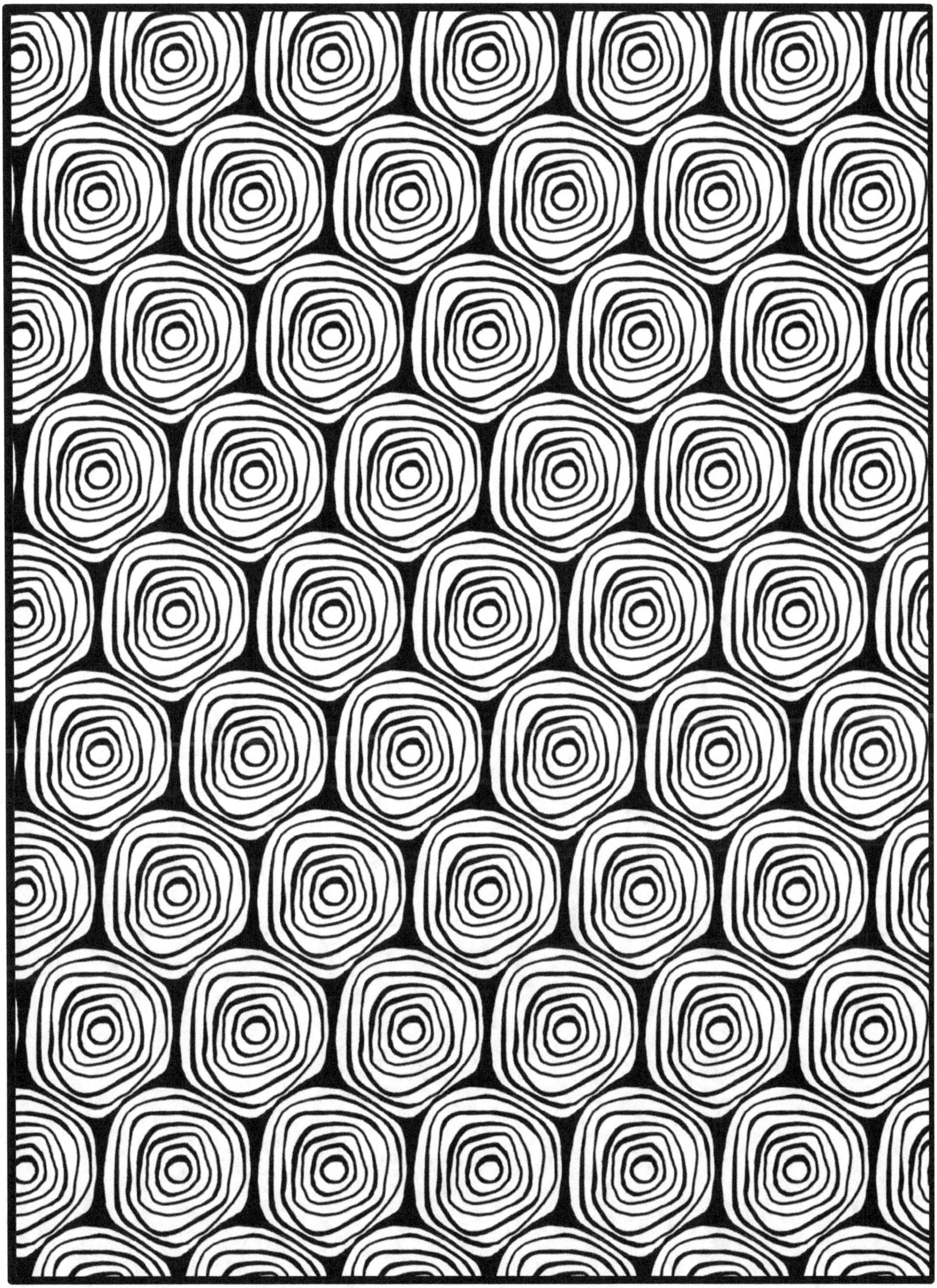

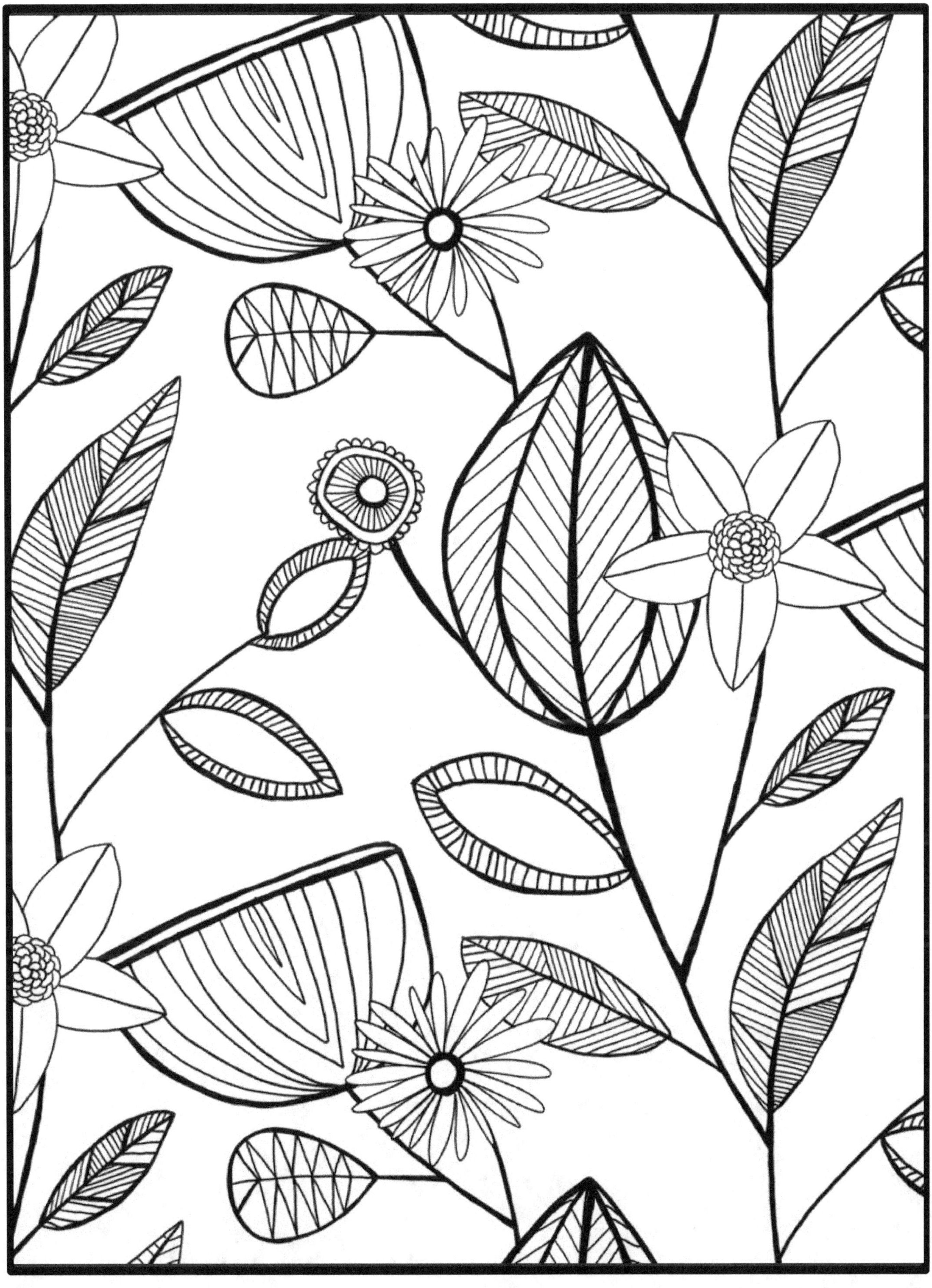

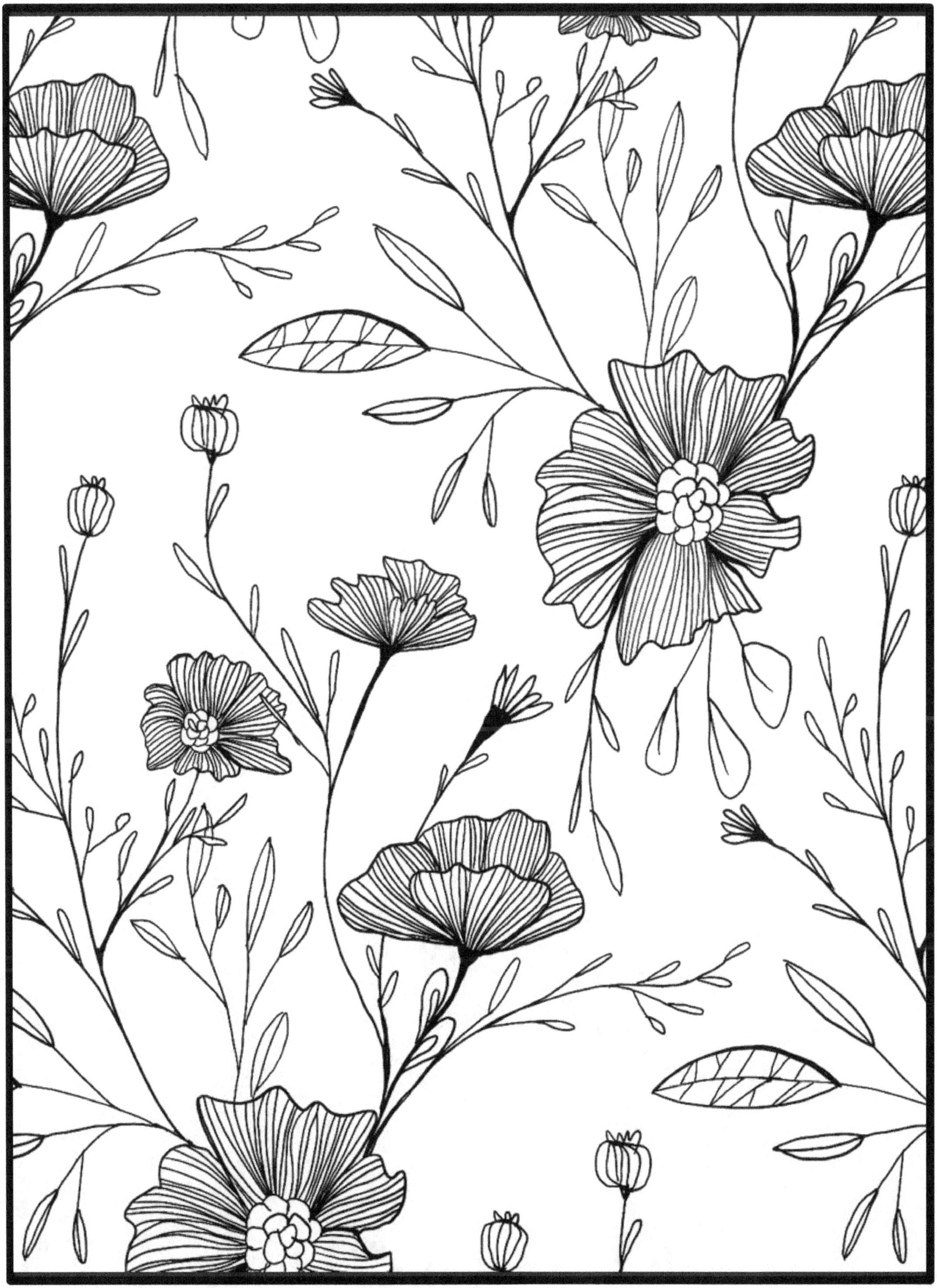

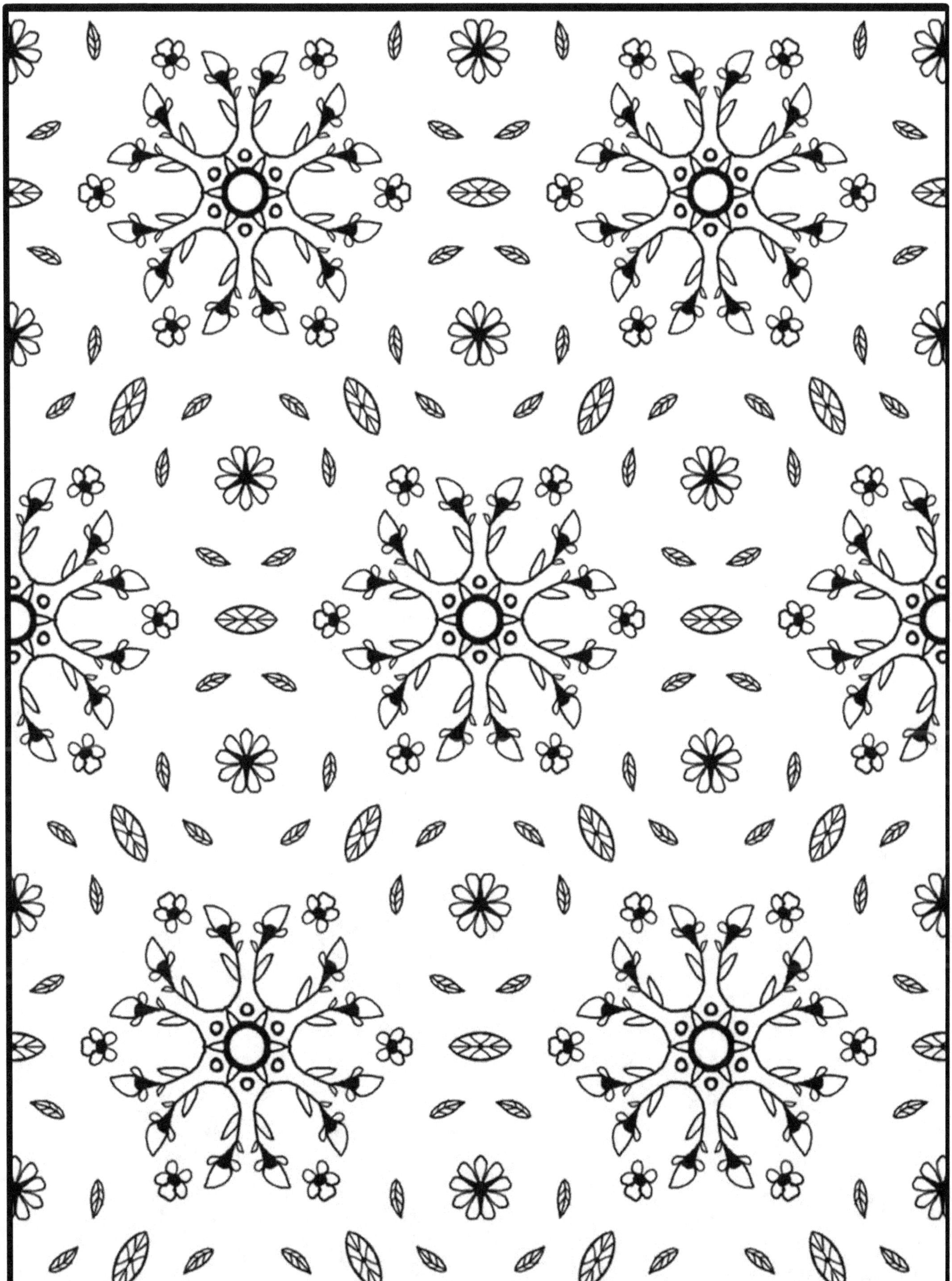

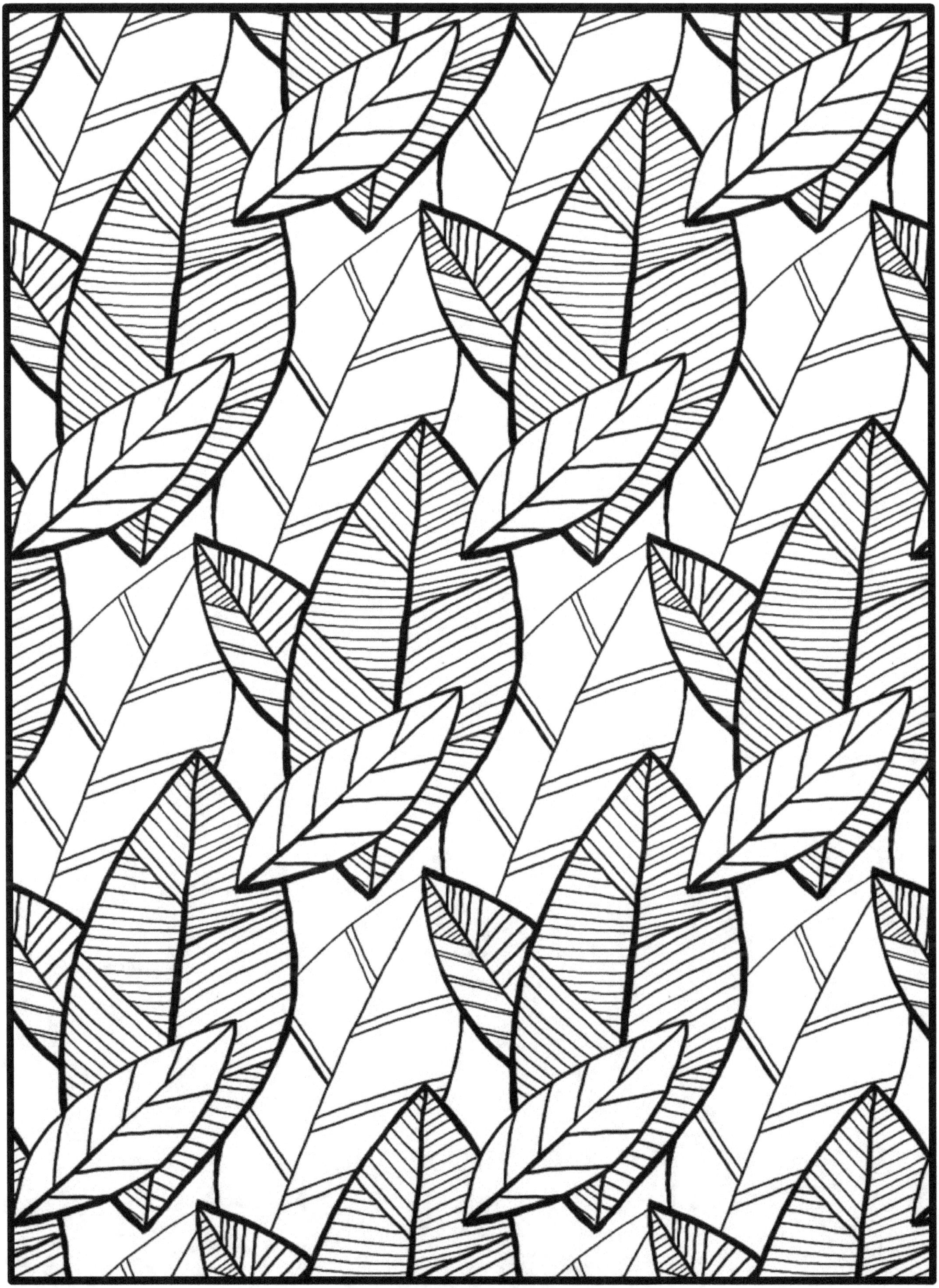

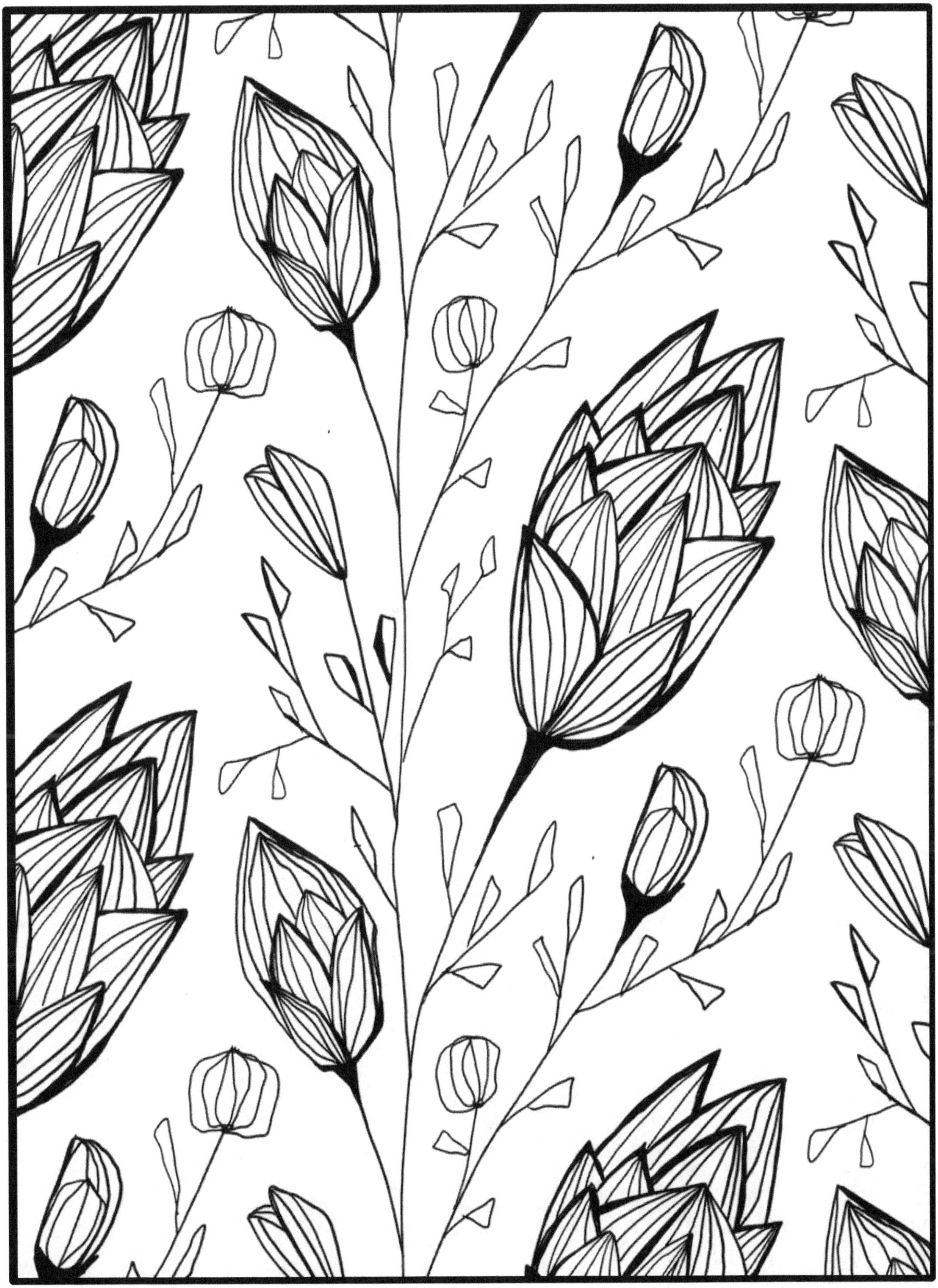

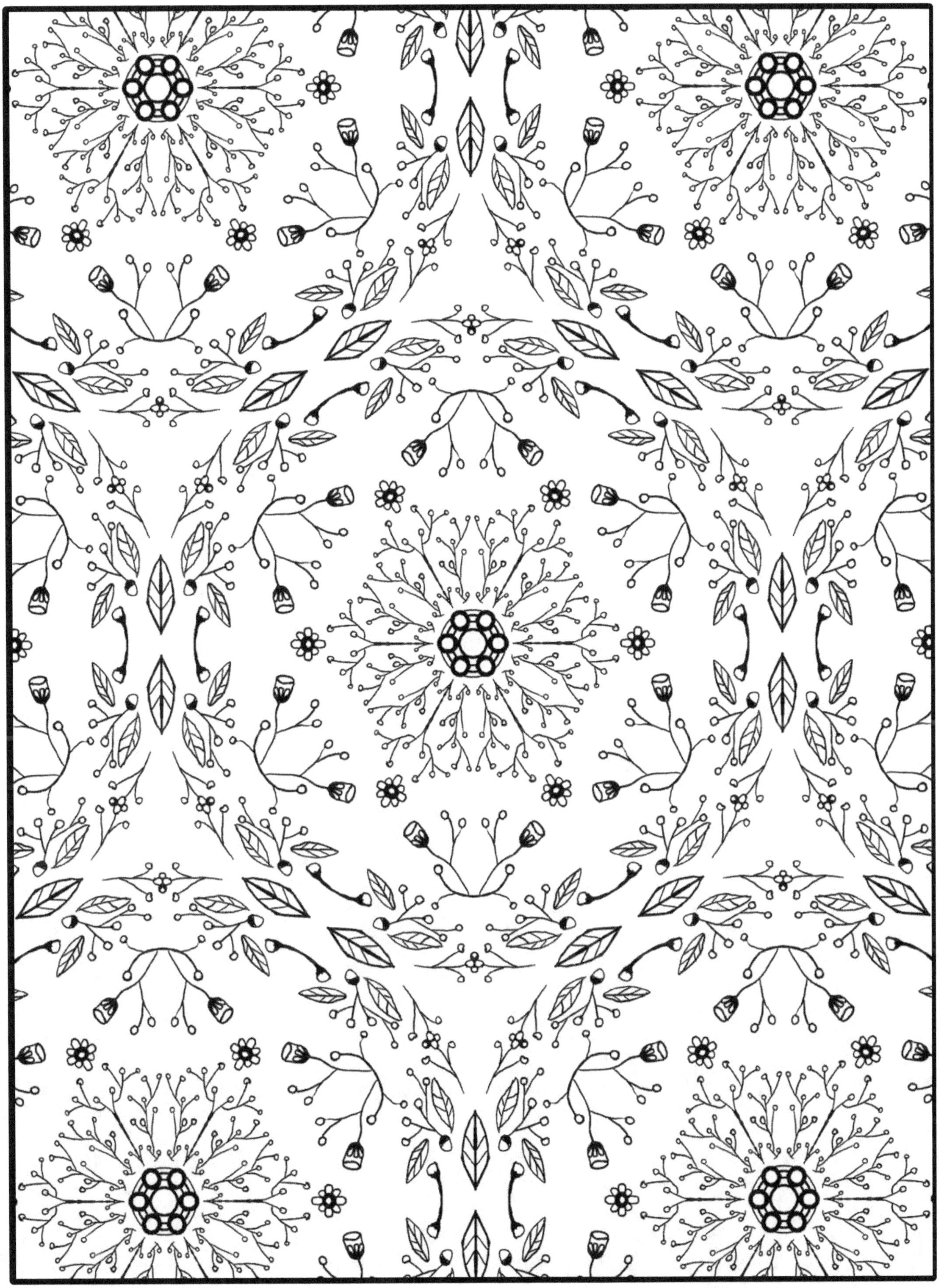

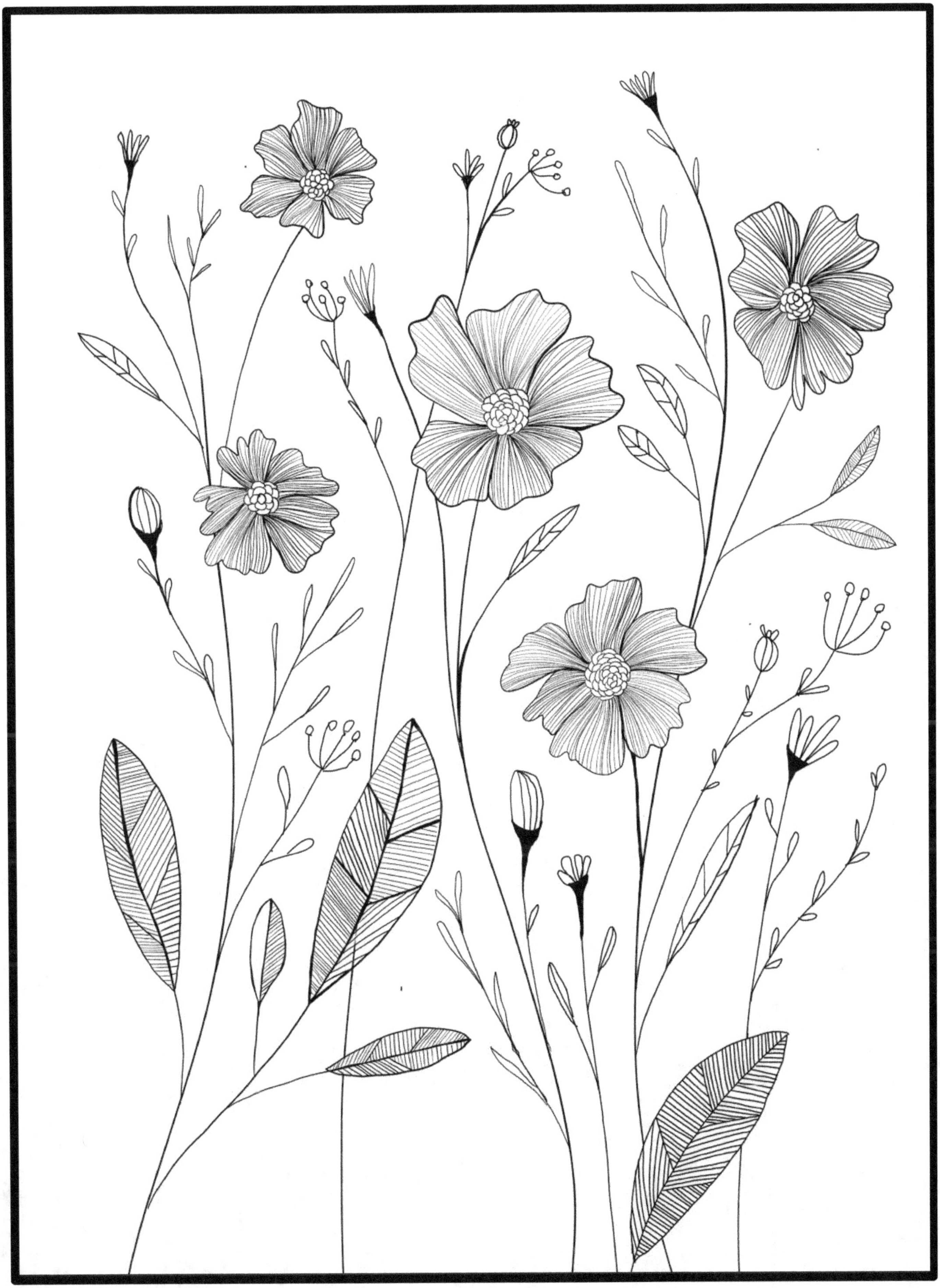

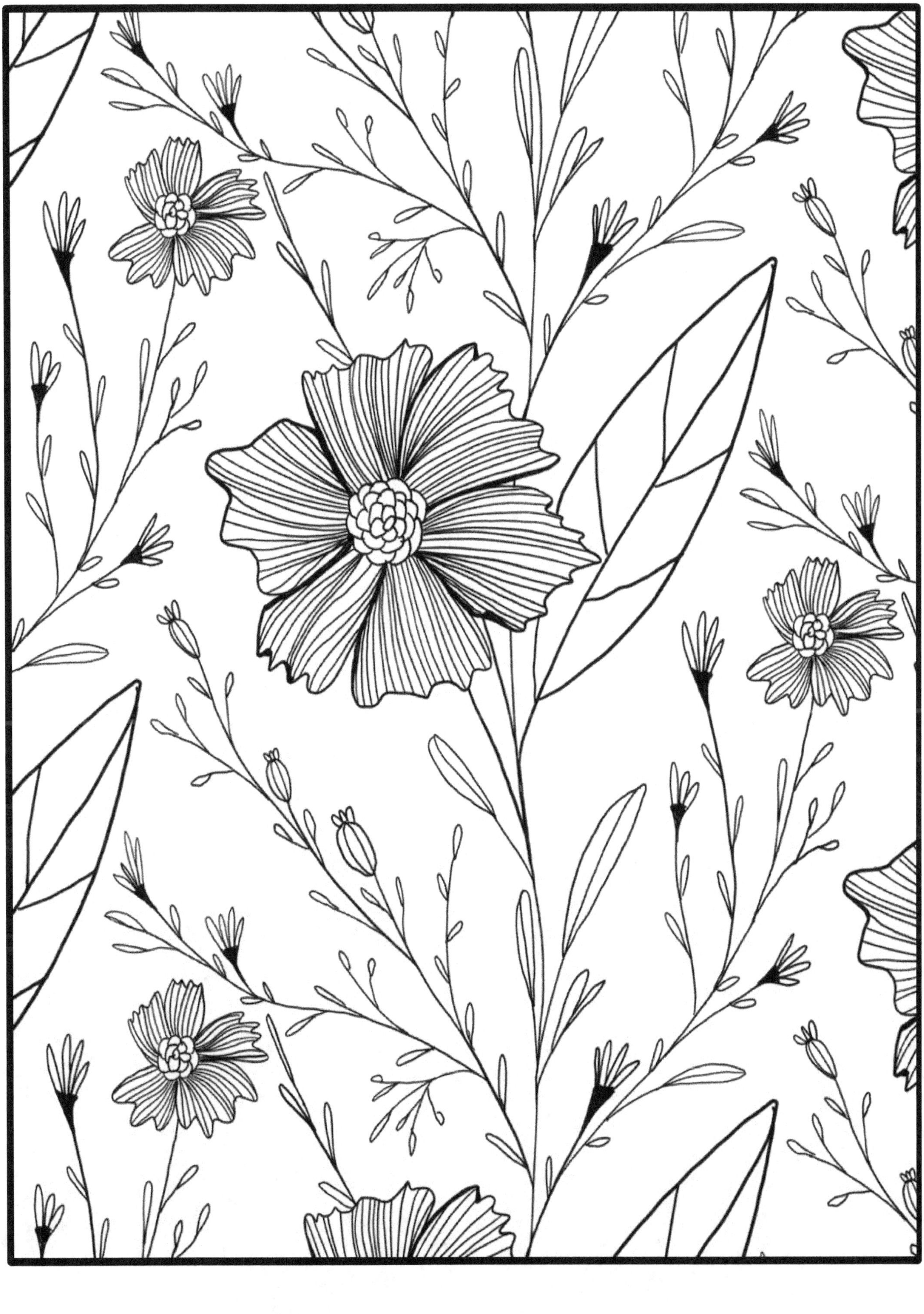

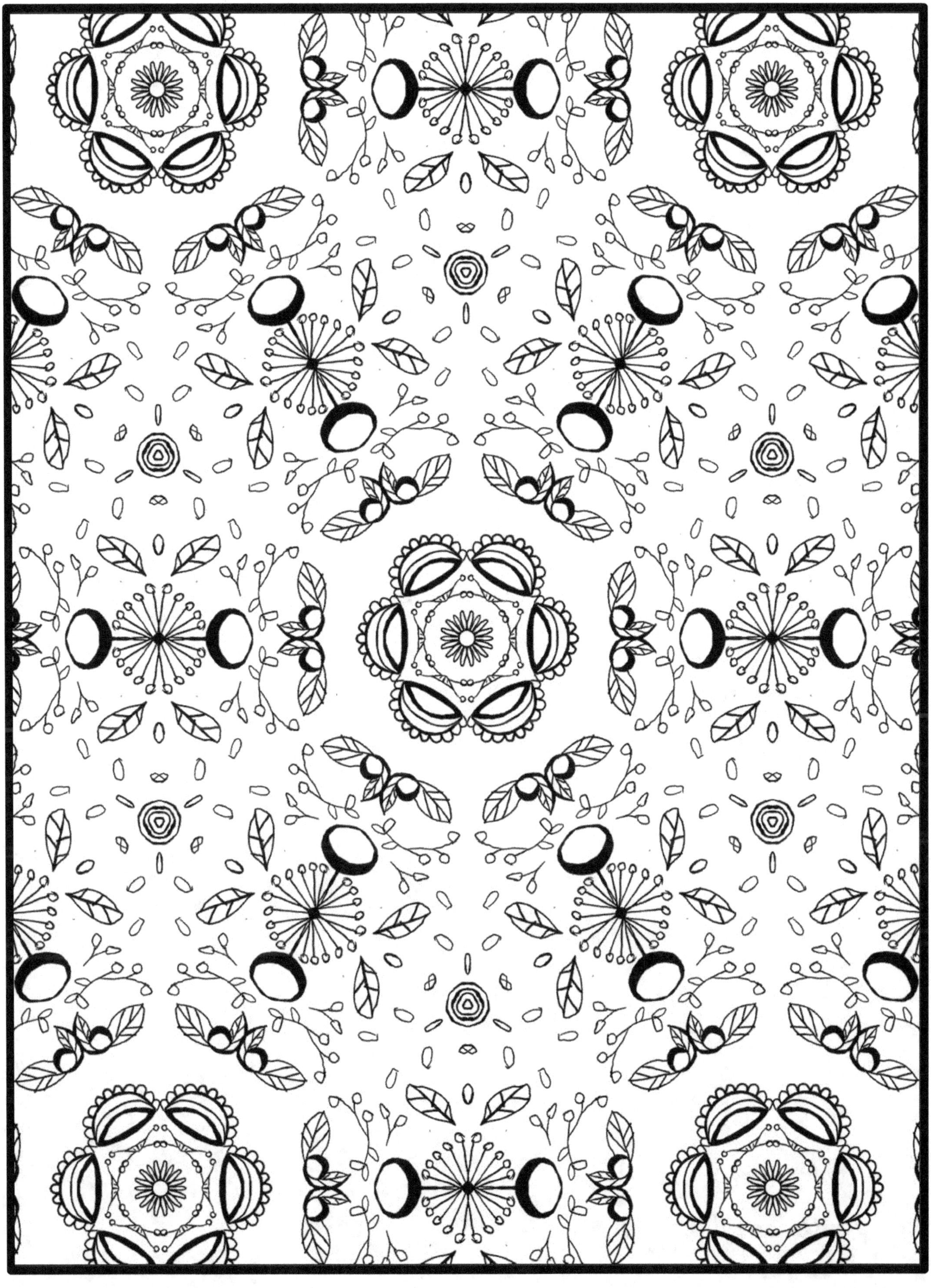

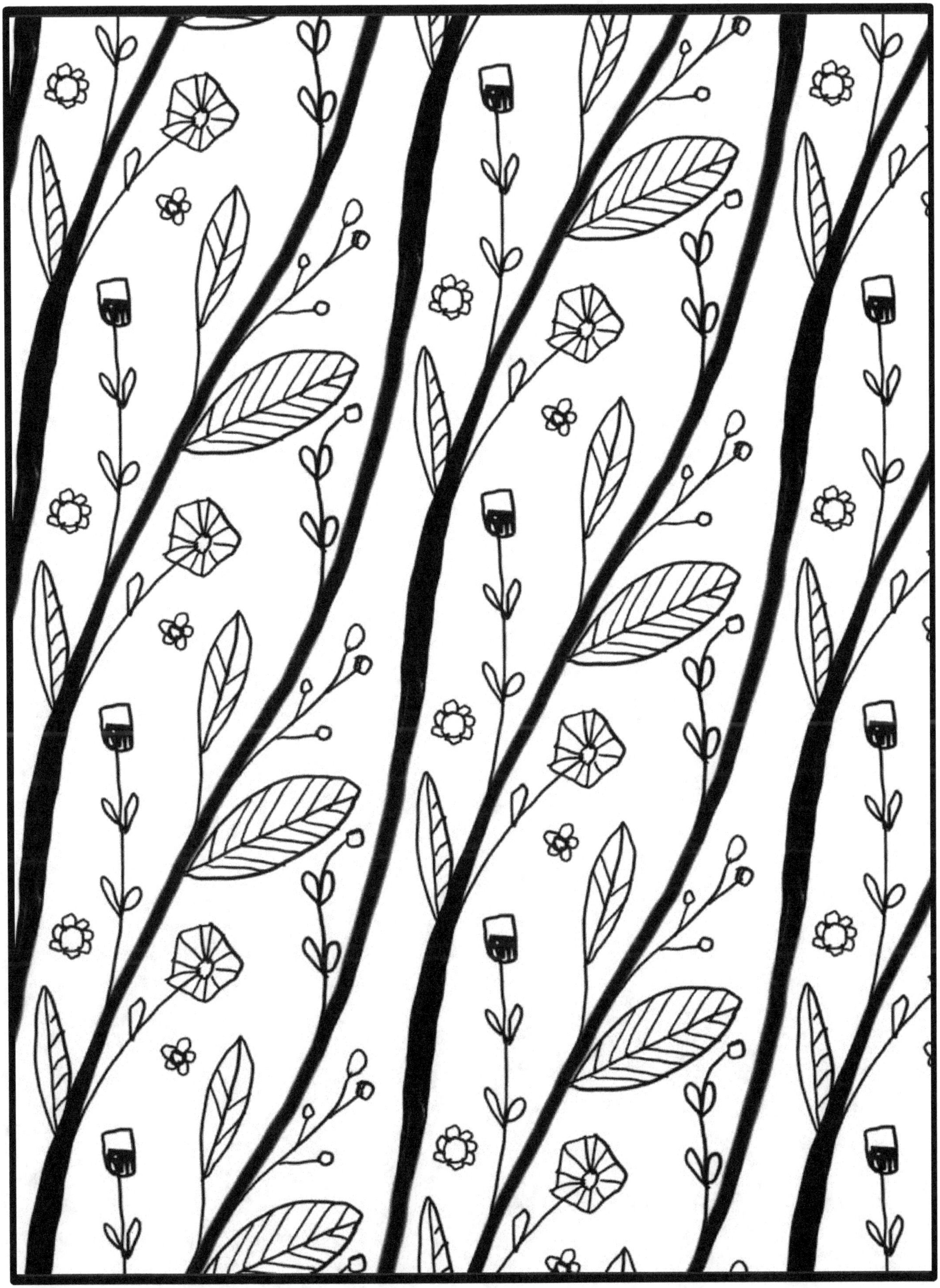

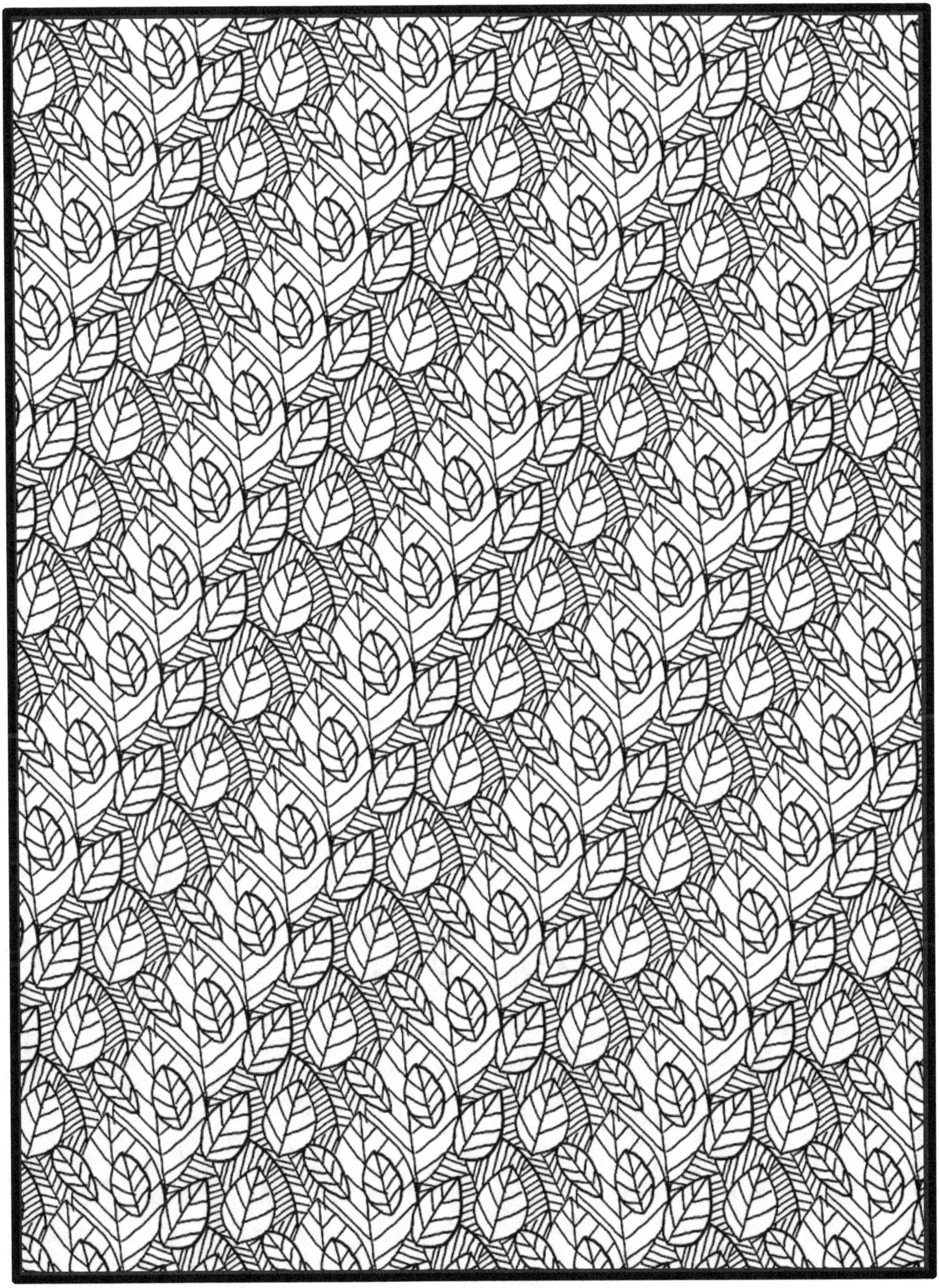

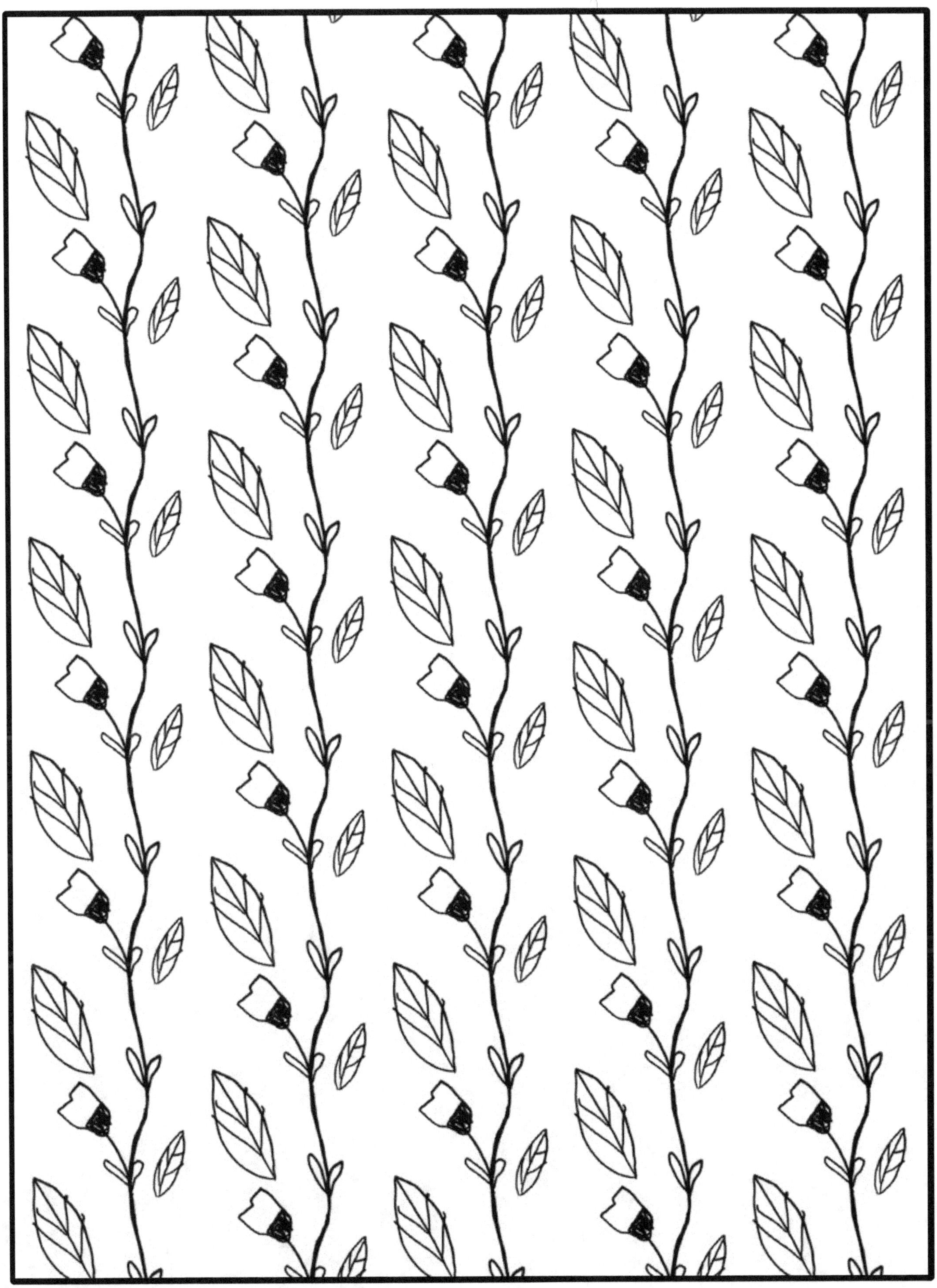

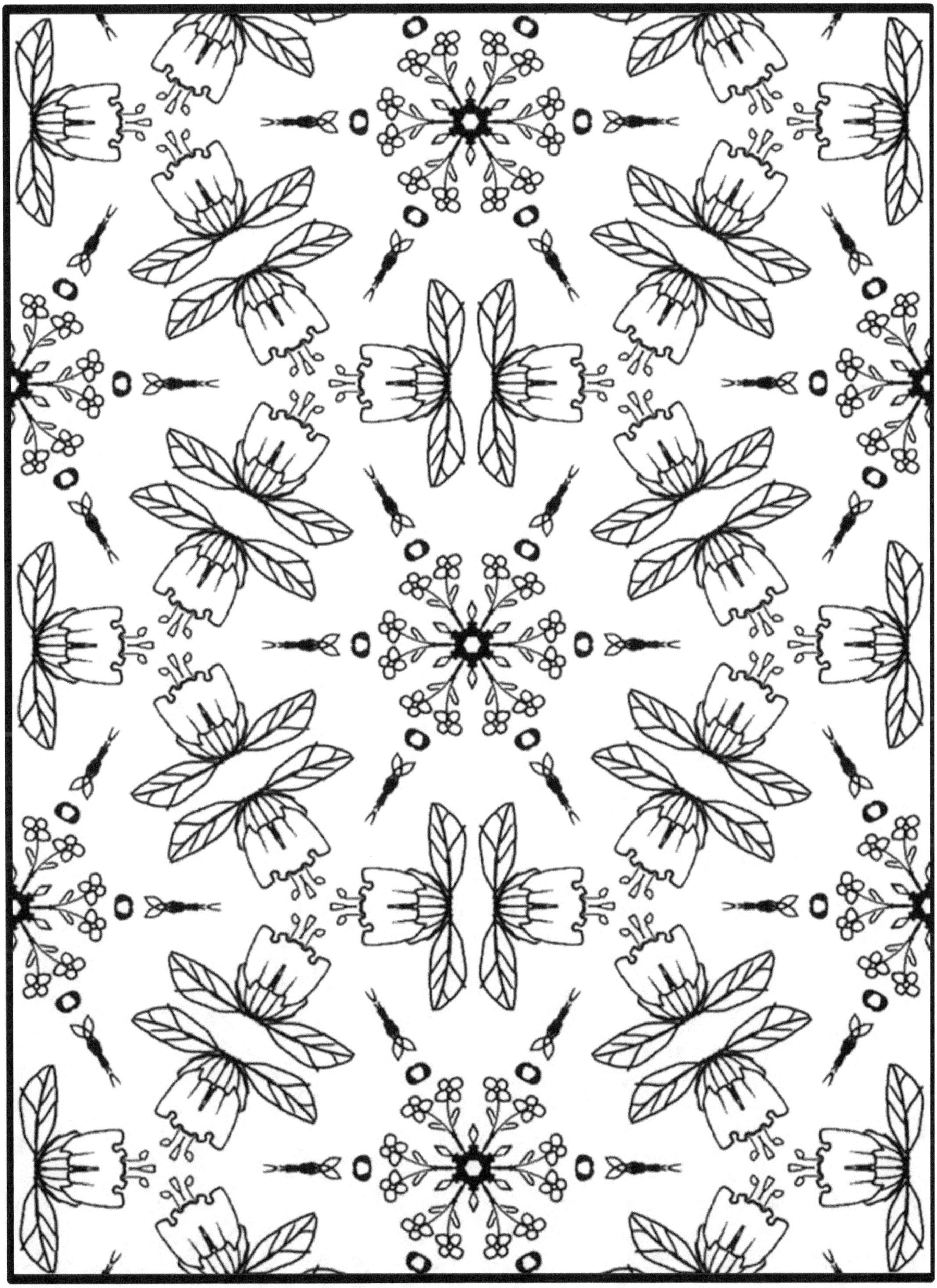

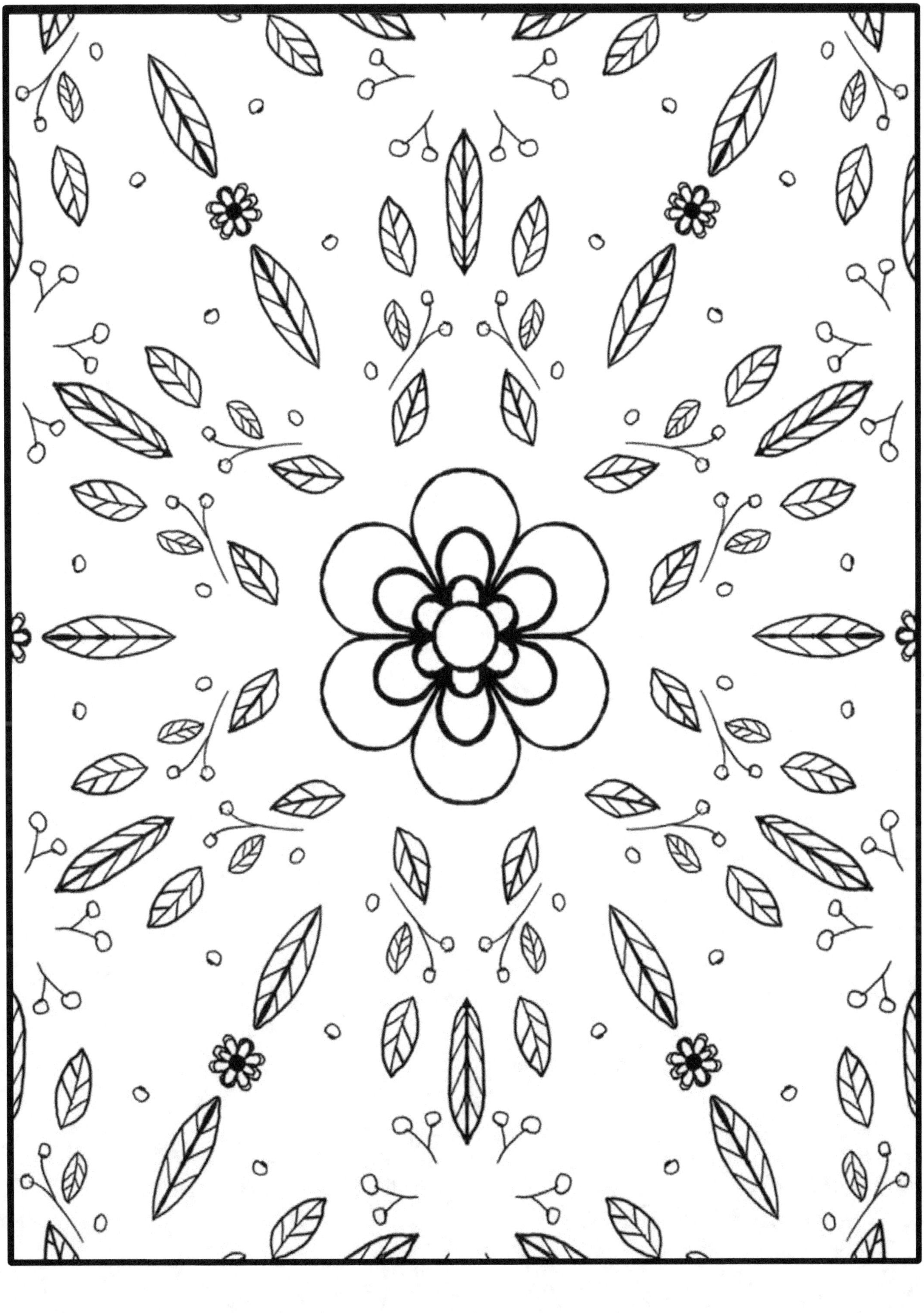

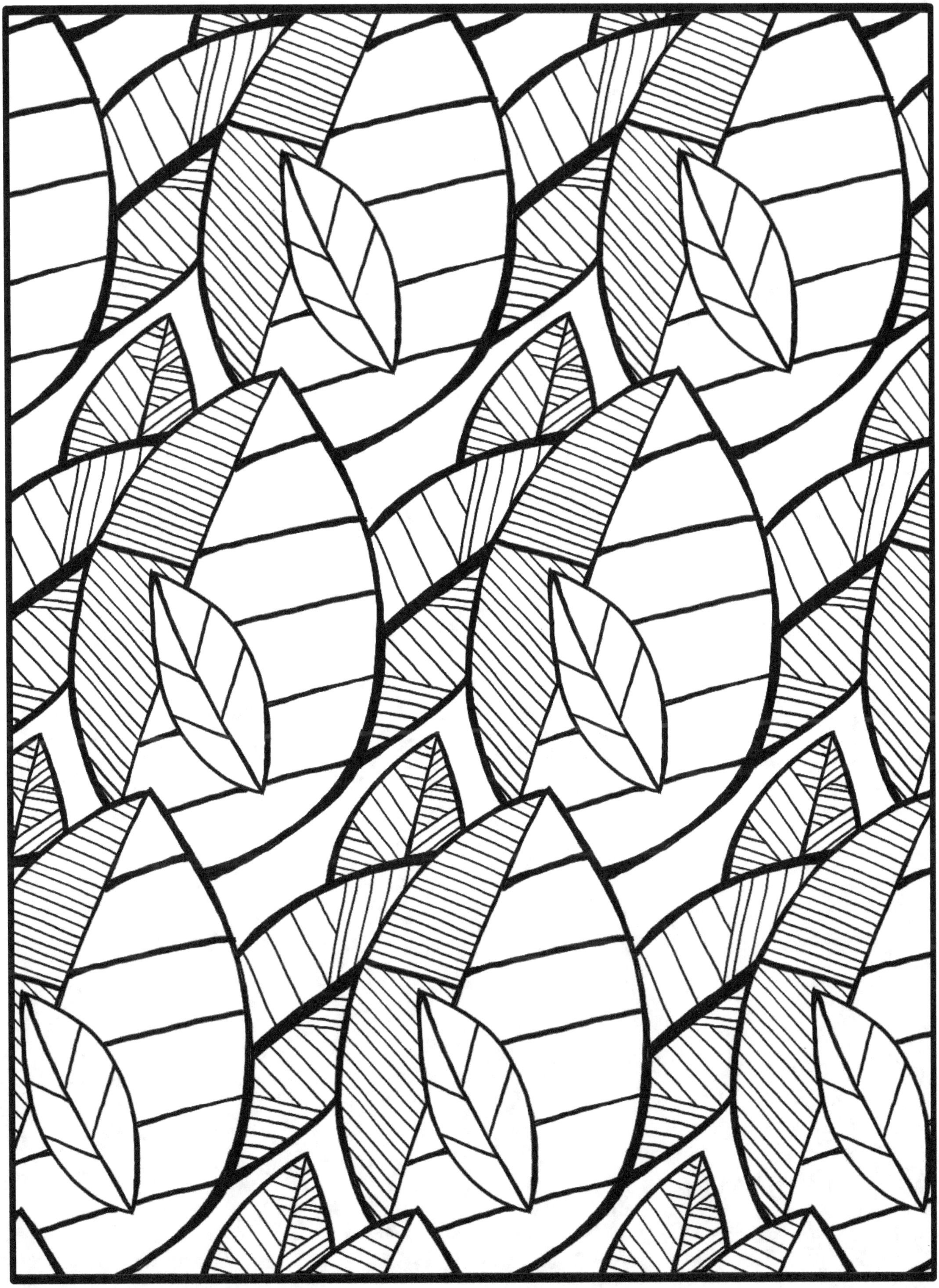

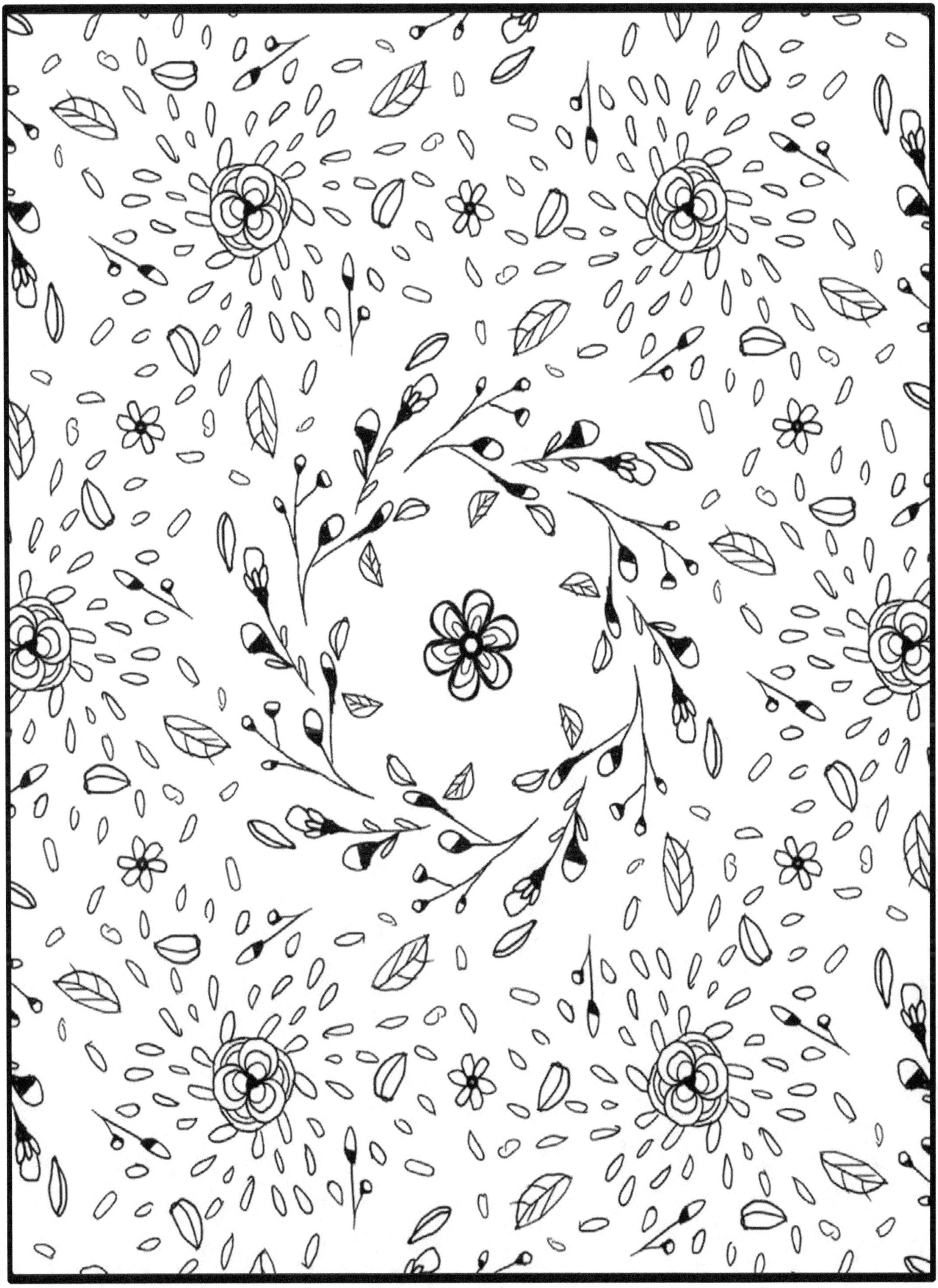

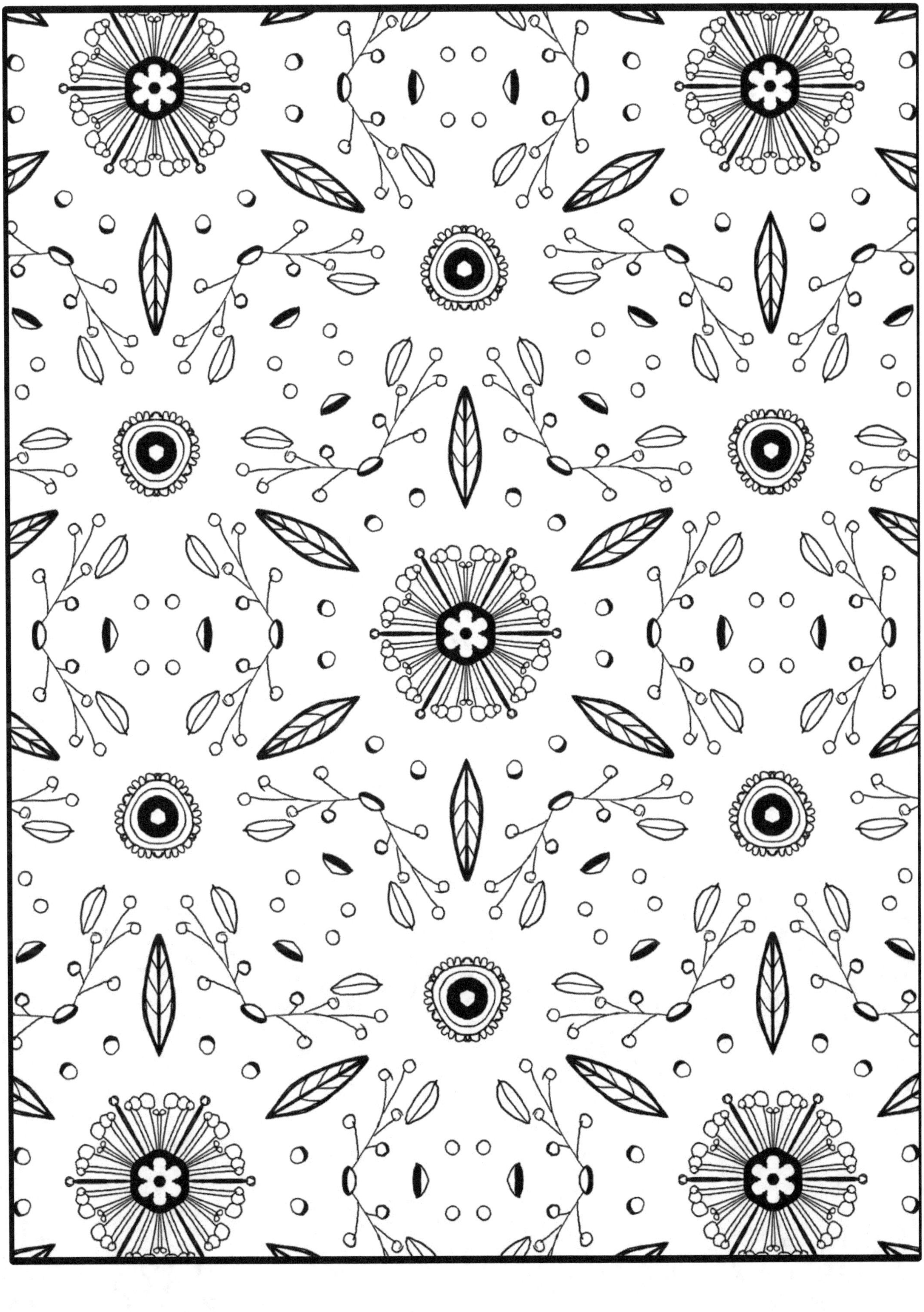

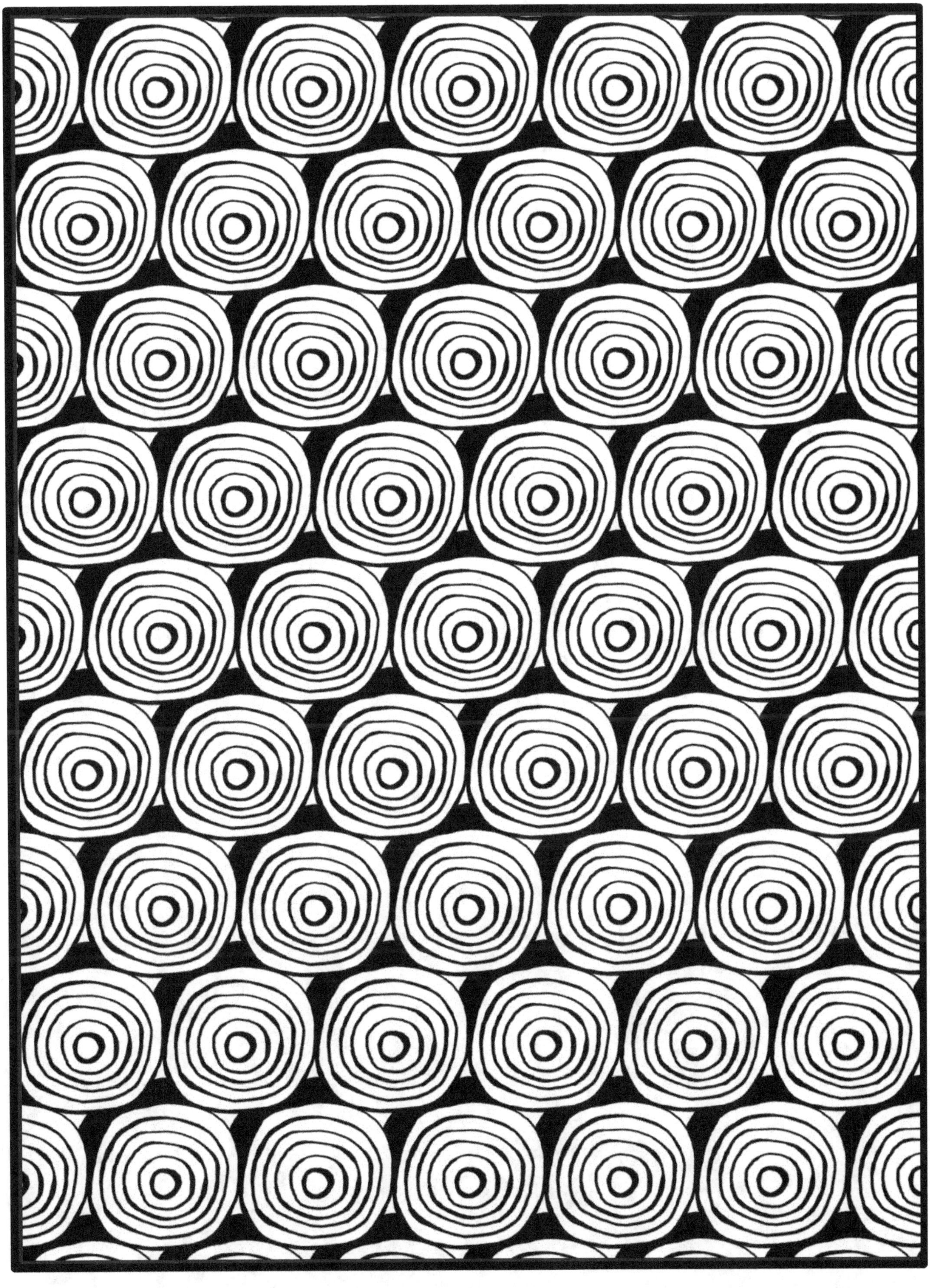

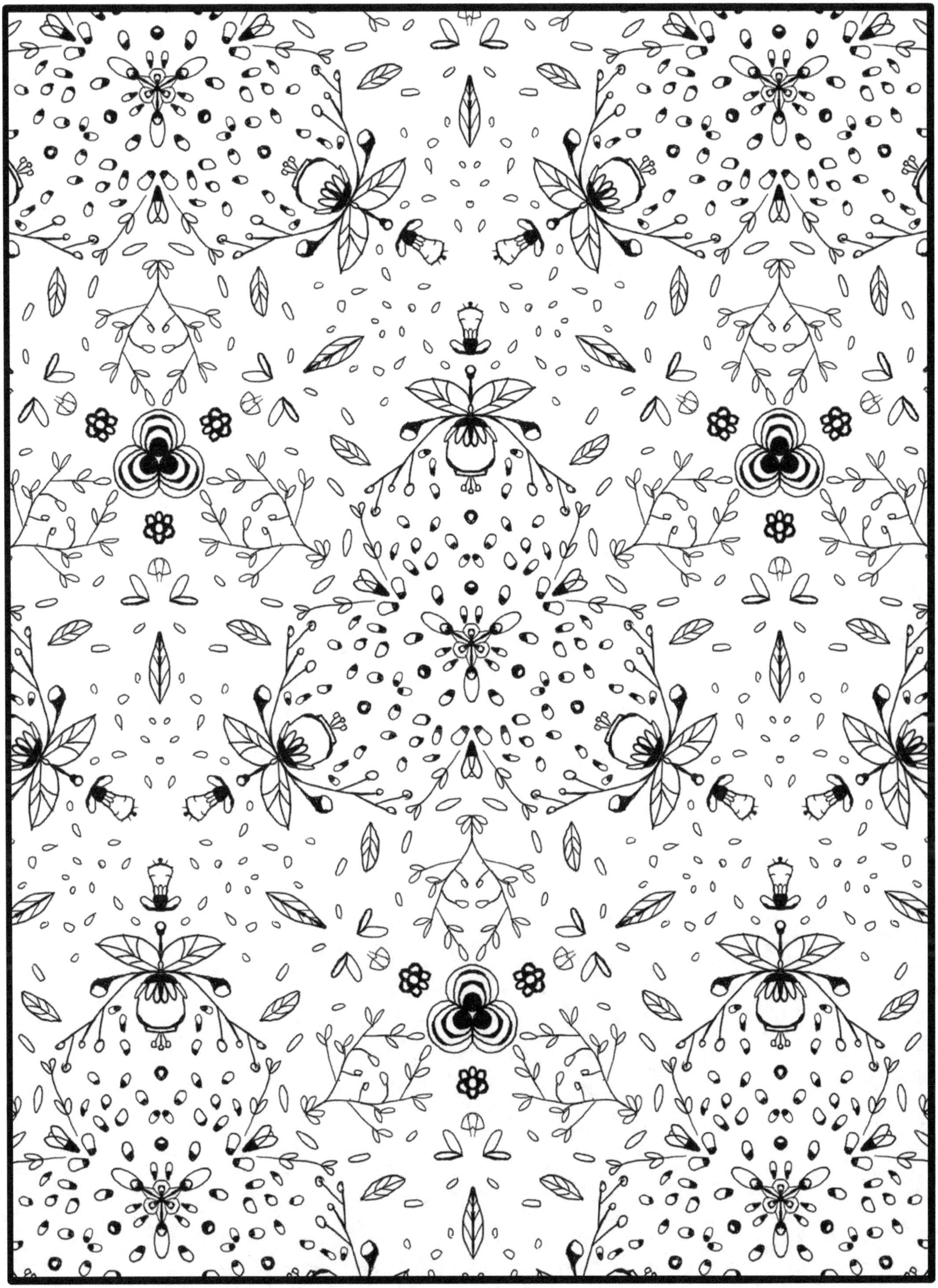

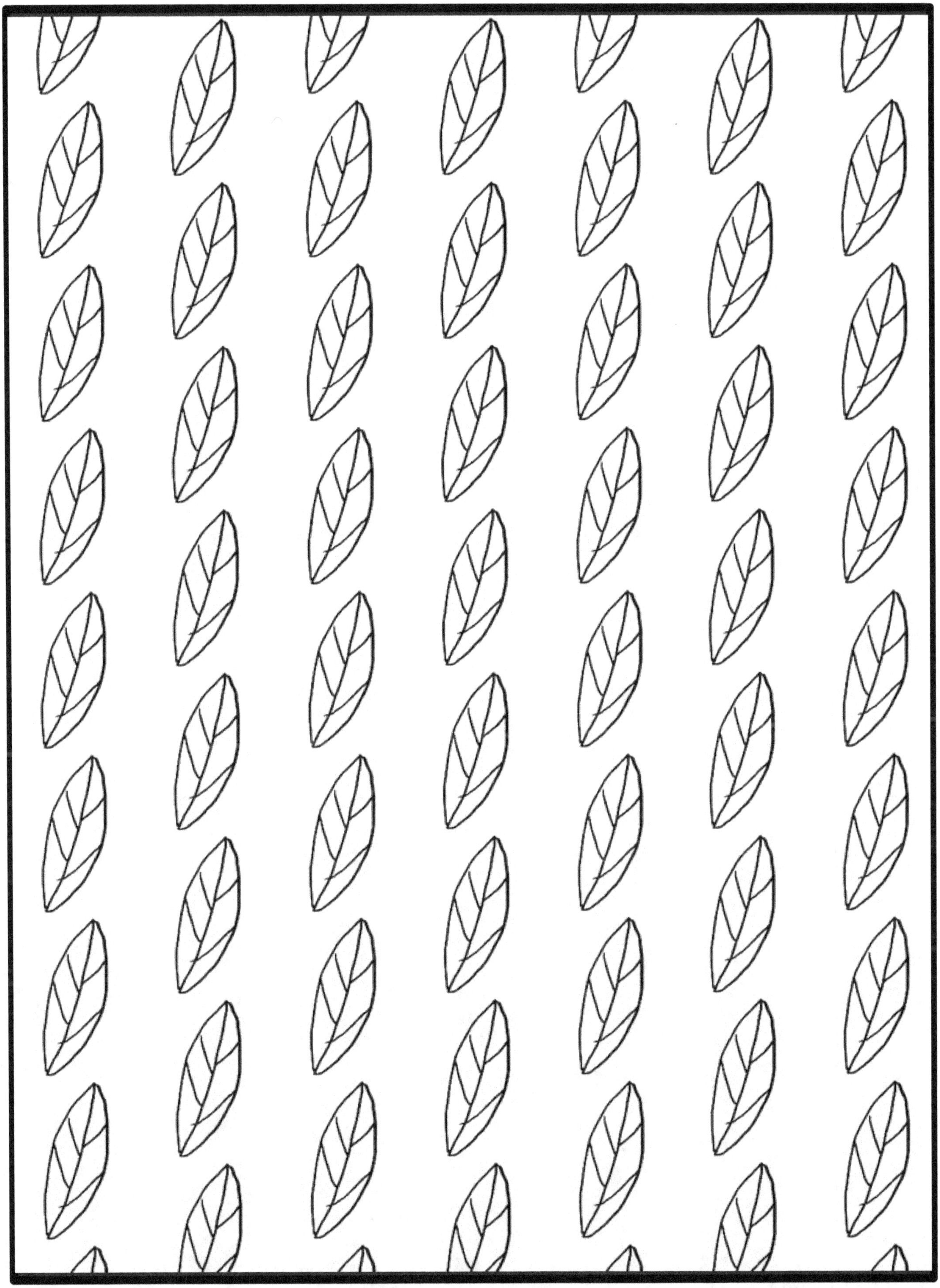

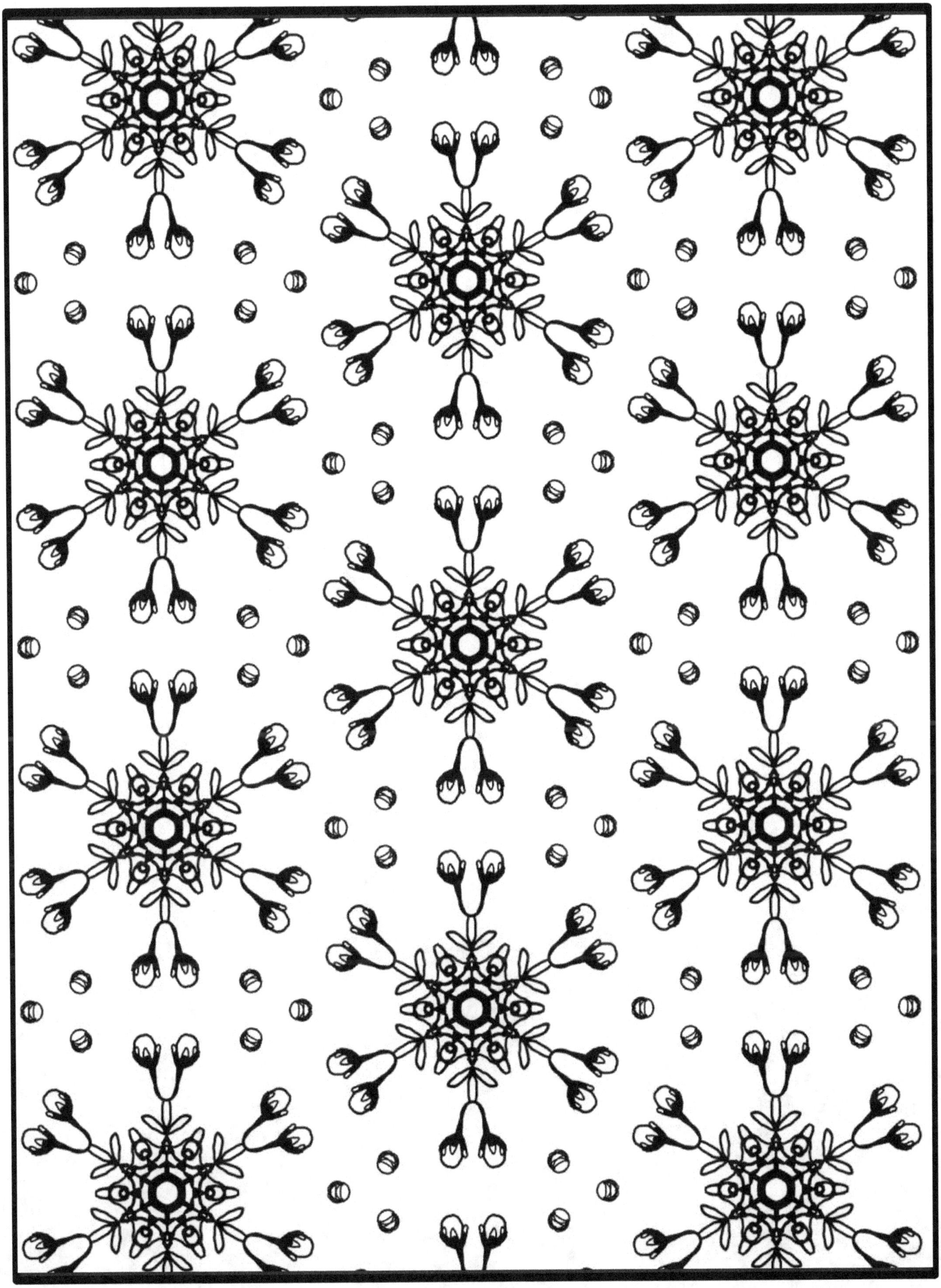

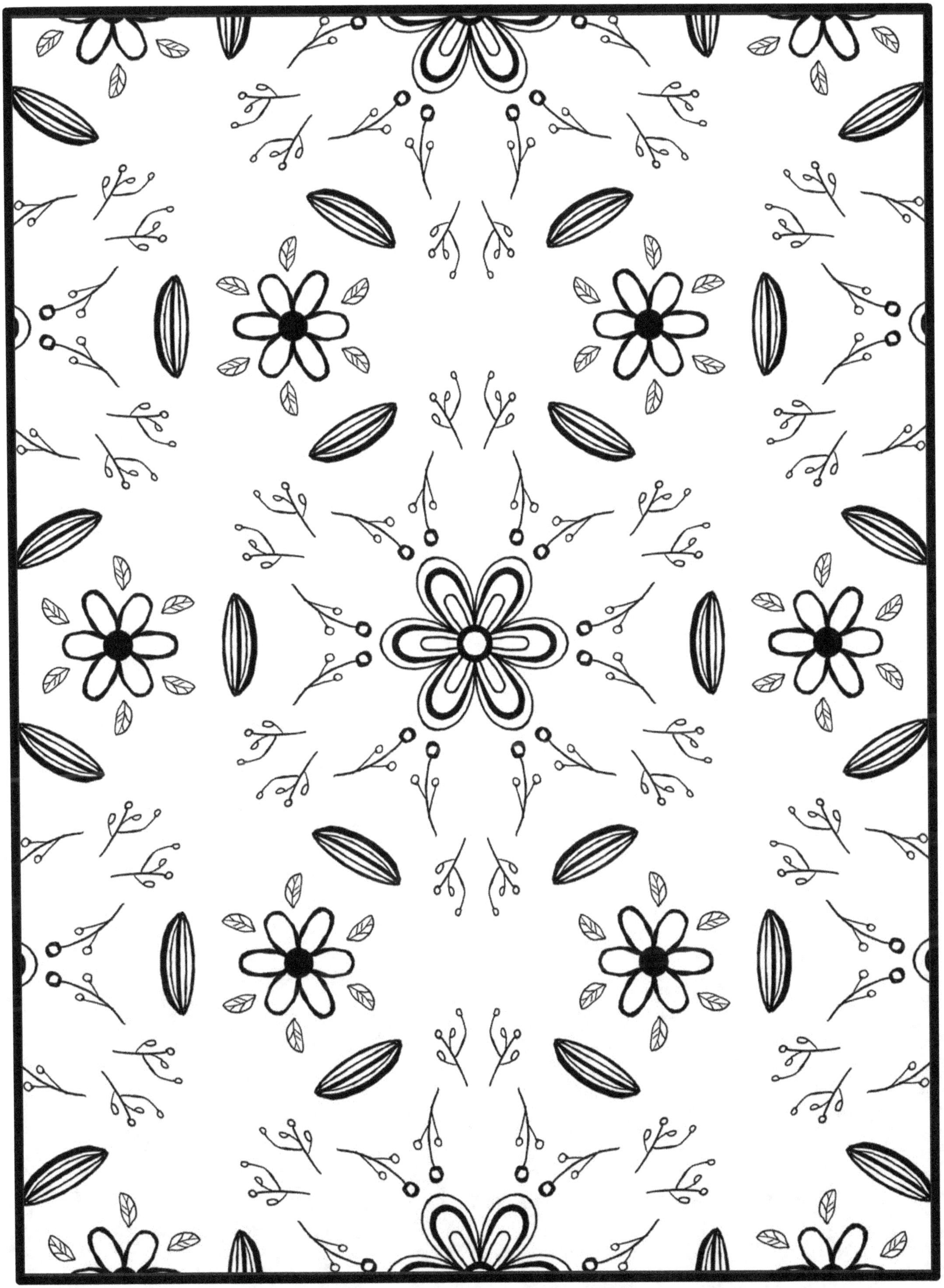

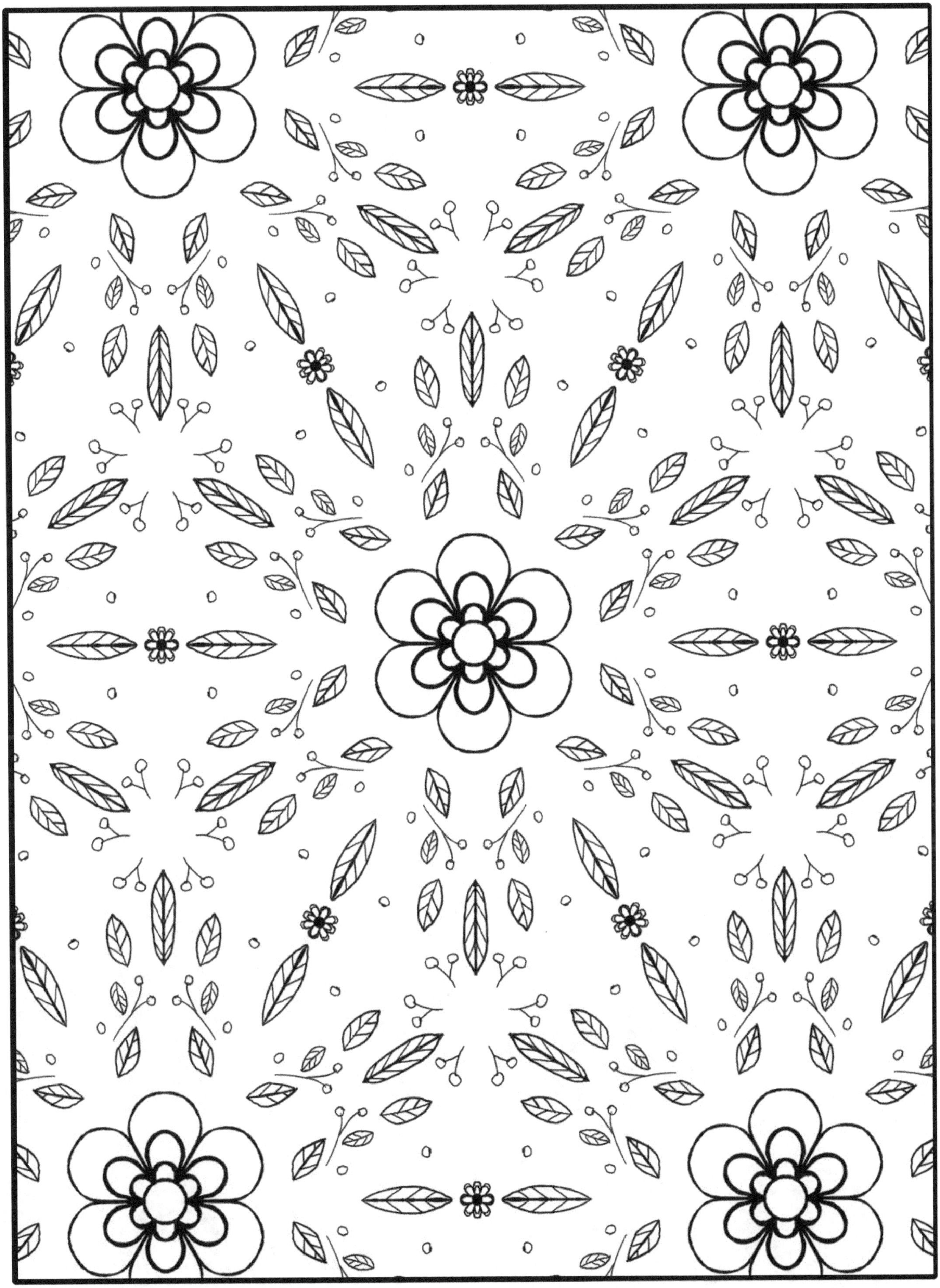

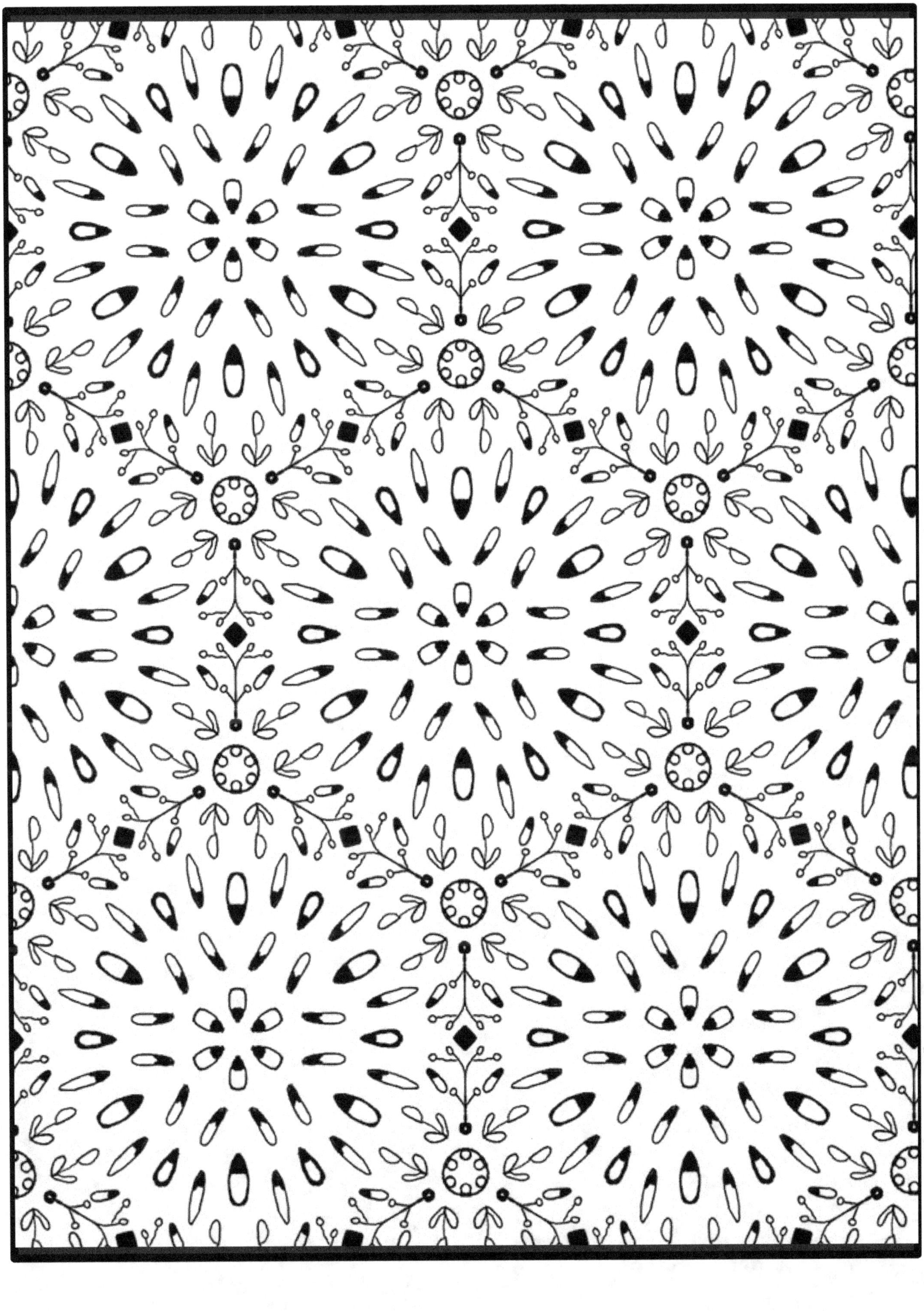

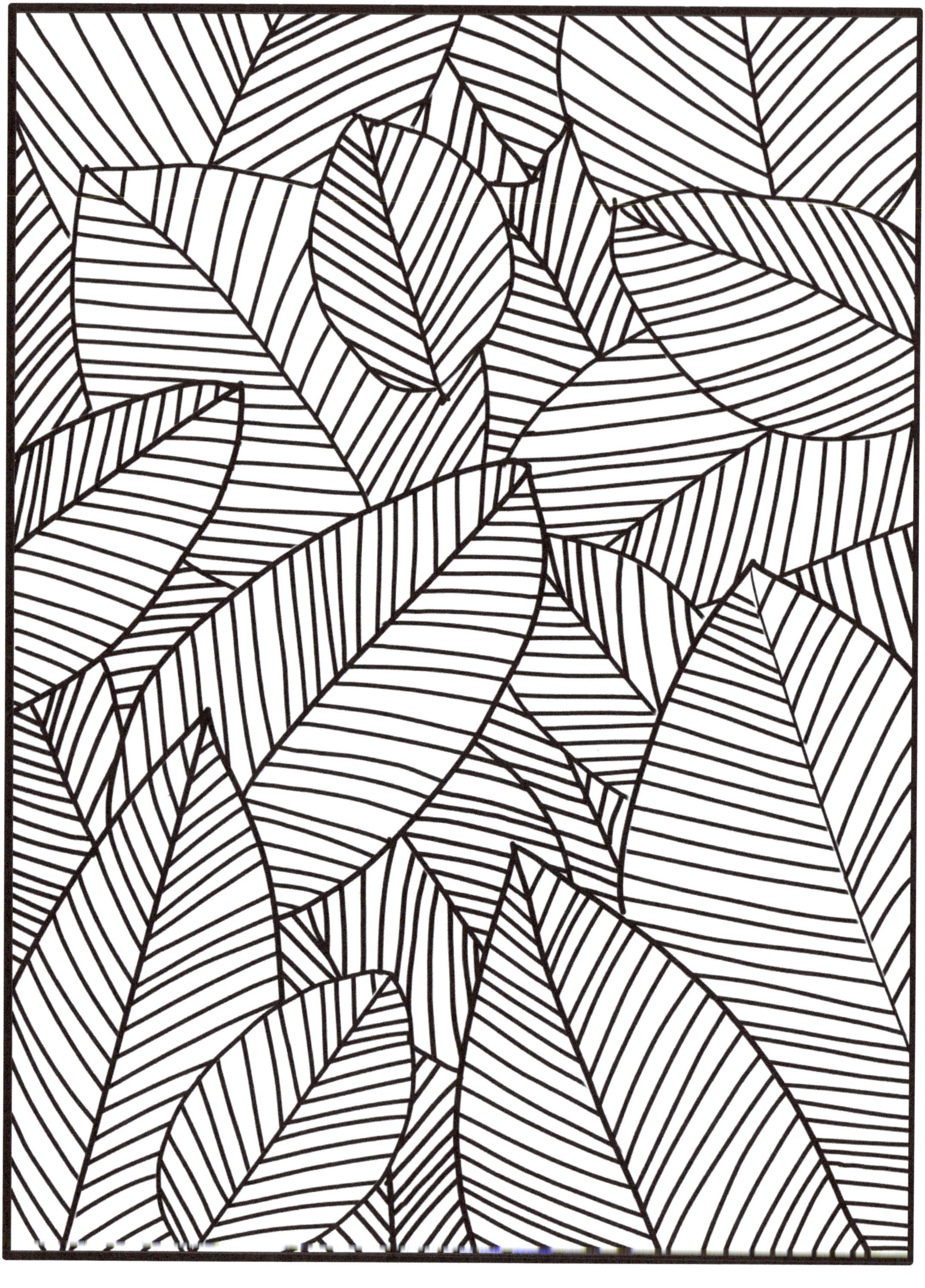

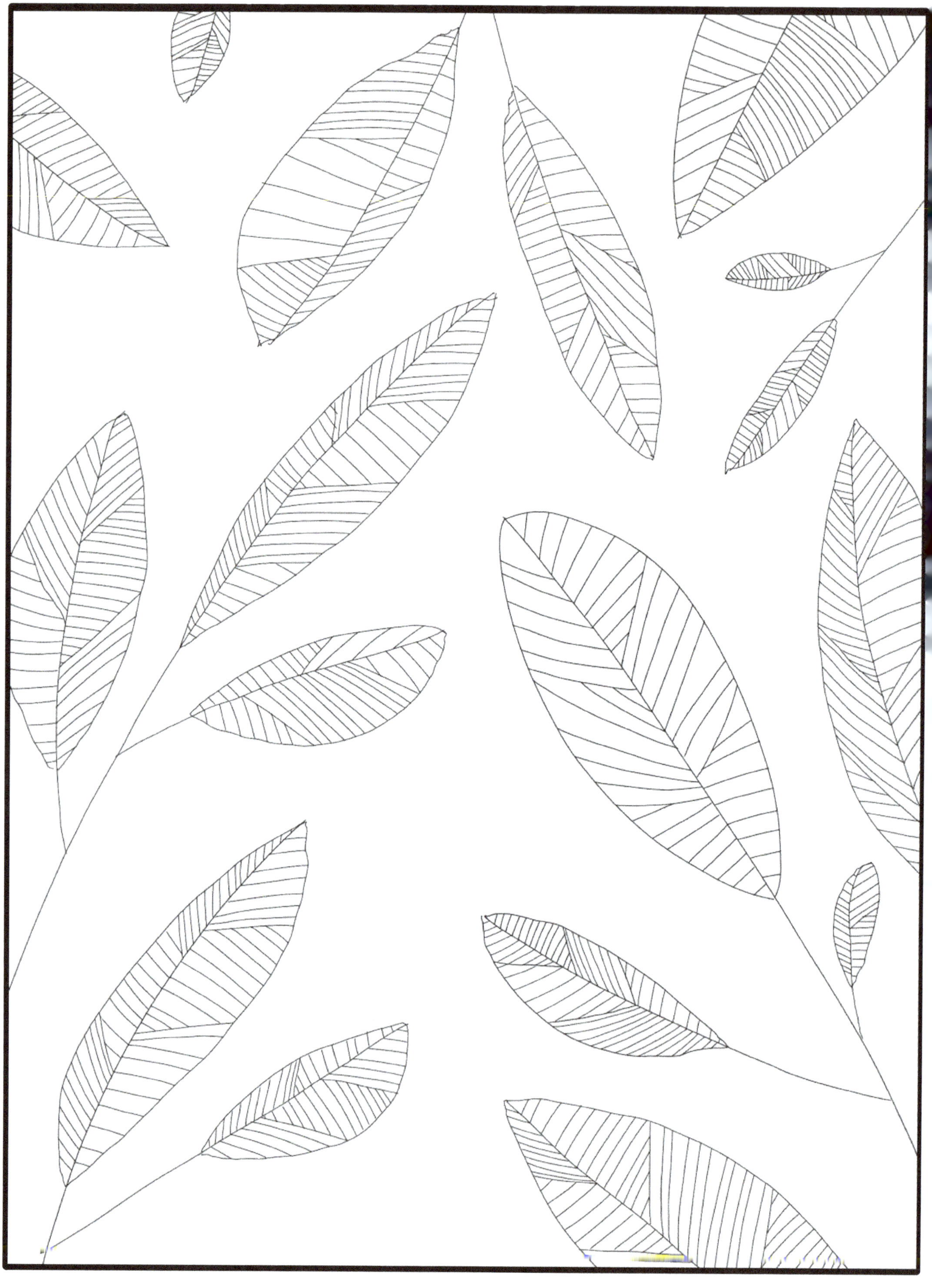

Color Test Page

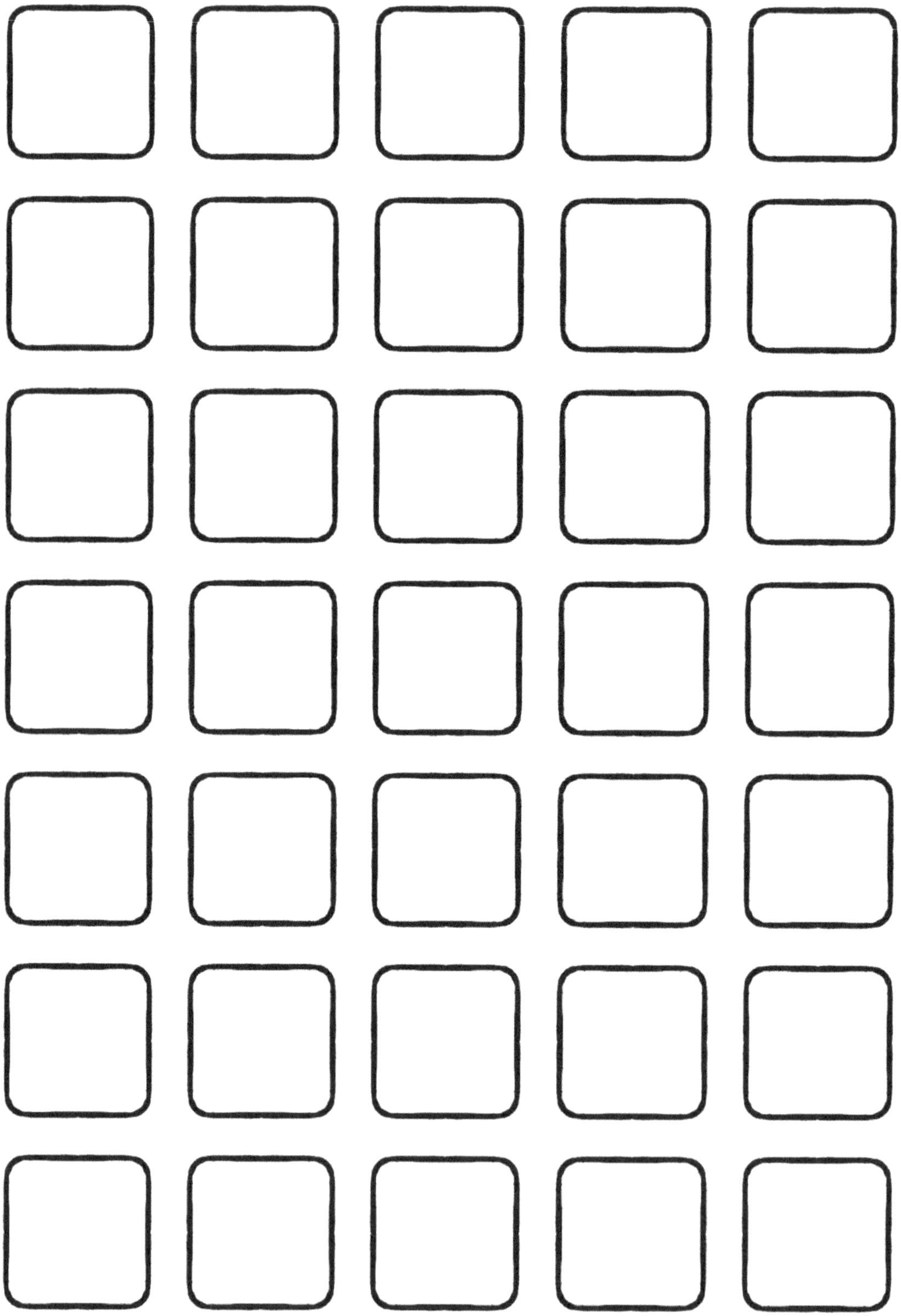

Color Test Page

www.ingramcontent.com/pod-product-compliance
Lightning Source LLC
Chambersburg PA
CBHW080519220526
45465CB00006B/2533
9798662792197